Christian
Personality
Under Construction

Though this book is designed for group study, it is also
intended for your personal enjoyment and spiritual
growth. A leader's guide is available from your local
bookstore or from your publisher.

Copyright 1988
Beacon Hill Press of Kansas City

Printed in the United States of America

Stephen M. Miller
Editor

Molly Mitchell
Editorial Assistant

Jack Mottweiler, *Chairman*
David Keith
Stephen Miller
Carl Pierce
Gene Van Note
Lyle Williams
Editorial Committee

Photo and Art Credits

Cover, Comstock; 5, 33, 71, 88, 118, reprinted with permission from the Saturday Evening Post Society, a division of BFL & MS, © 1985, 1986; 14, Strix Pix; 21, 81, Luke Golobitsh; 44, Steve and Mary Skjold; 54, Wallowitch; 64, 100, Masters Agency; 110, Bob Combs

12   11   10   9   8

Contents

Chapter 1

Improving Our Self-image

by David A. Seamands

Background Scripture: Proverbs 23:7; Romans 5:7-11; 1 John 3:1-2

MANY YEARS AGO, a famous plastic surgeon, Dr. Maxwell Maltz, wrote a best-selling book, *New Faces—New Futures*. It was a collection of case histories of people for whom facial plastic surgery had opened the door to a new life. The author's theme was that amazing personality changes can take place when a person's face is changed.

However, as the years went by, Dr. Maltz began to learn something else, not from his successes but from his failures. He began to see patient after patient who, even after facial plastic surgery, did not change. People who were made not simply acceptable, but actually beautiful, kept on thinking and acting the part of the ugly duckling. They acquired new faces but went on wearing the same old personalities. Worse than that, when they looked in a mirror, they would angrily exclaim to the doctor, "I look the same as before. You didn't change a thing." This, in spite of the fact that their friends and their family members could hardly recognize them.

In 1960 Dr. Maltz wrote his best-seller, *Psycho-Cybernetics* (Prentice-Hall). He was still trying to change people, not by correcting jutting jawbones, or smoothing out scars, but by helping them change the pictures they had of themselves.

Dr. Maltz says it is as if every personality has a face. This emotional face of personality seems to be the real key to change. If it remains scarred and distorted, ugly and inferior, then the person continues to act out a role, regardless of the change in his physical appearance. But if the face of his personality can be reconstructed, if the old emotional scars can be removed, the person can be changed.

All of us could confirm this by our experiences with people as well as our knowledge of ourselves. It is amazing

"The good news is that we've designed a computer
no bigger than a doughnut . . .
the bad news is that Hungerford dunked it in his coffee."

the way self-image influences our actions and attitudes, and especially our relationships with other people.

Take Marie, for example. Marie's husband, Jim, thought his wife was beautiful. He told me so before they ever came to talk things over. When I saw her, I agreed with him. Jim liked to brag on her to others, and never tired of lovingly telling Marie that she was beautiful. Now deep down, every wife wants this from her husband. But in Marie's case, her husband's admiration was causing problems, for Marie's picture of herself was diametrically opposite to what Jim saw.

"You're only saying that to flatter me," she'd say. "You don't really mean it."

Jim would feel hurt and frustrated. The more ways he tried to convince Marie that he really thought she was beautiful, the bigger the barrier became.

"I know what I look like," she said. "I can see myself in the mirror. You don't have to make up things like that. Why don't you love me for what I am?" And round and round it went.

Marie's self-concept kept her from thanking God for the gift of beauty. It prevented her from seeing reality. Worst of all, it hindered her from developing a beautiful love-gift relationship with her devoted husband.

What is self-image or self-concept? Your self-image is based on a whole system of pictures and feelings you have put together about yourself. Nowhere is the biblical statement about the heart and mind more appropriate than here: "As he thinketh in his heart, so is he" (Proverbs 23:7, KJV). The way you *look at* yourself and *feel about* yourself, way down deep in the heart of your personality—so you will be and so you will become. What you see and feel will determine your relationships both with other people and with God.

Dr. Maurice Wagner, a professional Christian counselor, in his excellent book *The Sensation of Being Somebody*

(Zondervan, pp. 32-37), explains the three essential components of a healthy self-image:

The first is *a sense of belongingness,* of being loved. This is simply the awareness of being wanted, accepted, cared for, enjoyed, and loved. I personally believe that this sense begins before birth. I've counseled people with such deep wounds that I am convinced their sense of rejection traces back to their parents' attitudes before birth. If a child is unwanted, rarely will he have a sense of belonging.

The second component is *a sense of worth and value.* This is the inner belief and feeling: "I count. I am of value. I have something to offer."

The third is *a sense of being competent.* It is the feeling-concept: "I can do this task; I can cope with that situation; I am able to meet life." Put them all together, Dr. Wagner says, and you have a triad of self-concept feelings: belongingness, worthwhileness, and competence.

A person's self-concept is a system of feelings and concepts he has constructed about himself. There are four sources from which we get our self-concepts.

• The first is the *outer world.* From this outer world we see pictures and feelings about ourselves reflected in the mirrors of family members. We decide who we are from our earliest system of relationships—by how we are treated and loved and cared for, and the language of relationships that we learn as we are growing up.

Do you remember the last time you went into the house of mirrors in an amusement park? You looked in one mirror and saw yourself as tall and skeletal, with foot-long hands. In the next one, you were round like a big balloon. Another mirror combined both, so that from the waist up you looked like a giraffe, while from the waist down you looked like a hippopotamus.

Looking into the mirrors was a hilarious experience, especially for the person standing next to you. He was just knocked out at how funny you looked. What was happening? The mirrors were so constructed that you saw yourself according to the curvature of the glass.

Now, move those mirrors over into the family. What if somehow your mother, your dad, your brother, your sister, your grandparents, the important others in your early life— what if they had taken every mirror in the house and curved them a certain way, so that in every mirror you saw a distorted reflection of yourself? What would have happened? It wouldn't have taken you long to develop an image of yourself just like the one you were seeing in the family mirrors. After a while you would have begun talking and acting and relating to people in a way that would have fit the picture you kept seeing in those mirrors.

• The second source is the *world within us,* the physical, emotional, and spiritual equipment that we bring into the world. This includes our senses, our nerves, our capacity to learn, to register, to respond. For some of us, the world within includes handicaps, deformities, and defects.

God has revealed to us in His Word that we do not enter this life morally neutral. Rather, we are victims of a basic tendency toward evil, a proclivity toward the wrong. We call it original sin. We do not come into this world perfectly neutral, but imperfectly weighted in the direction of the wrong. We are out of balance in our motives, desires, and drives. We are out of proportion, with a bent toward the wrong. And because of this defect in our natures, our responses are off-center.

The Bible makes it clear that we are not merely victims. We all are sinners and share in the responsibility of who we are and what we are becoming. I have never seen anyone truly healed of low self-esteem until, along with forgiving all those who hurt and wronged him, he also received God's forgiveness for his own wrong responses.

• *Satan* is a third source. Satan uses our feelings of self-despising as a terrible weapon in three roles that he plays. Satan is a liar (John 8:44), the accuser (Revelation 12:10), and the one who blinds our minds (2 Corinthians 4:4). In all three roles he uses inferiority, inadequacy, and self-belittling to defeat Christians and prevent them from realizing their full potential as God's own children.

• The fourth source for our self-concept is *God.* We now move from the problem of low self-image to the power for a new Christian self-image. We now turn away from the disease to its cure, for there are practical steps you can take toward the healing of your low self-esteem.

Take Your Self-estimate from God

Develop the picture of your worth and value from God, not from the false reflections that come out of your past. The healing of low self-esteem really hinges on a choice you must make: Will you listen to Satan as he employs all the lies, the distortions, the put-downs, and the hurts of your past to keep you bound by unhealthy, unchristian feelings and concepts about yourself? Or will you receive your self-esteem from God and His Word?

Here are some very important questions to ask yourself.

• *What right have you to belittle or despise someone whom God loves so deeply?* Don't say, "Well, I know God loves me, but I just can't stand myself." That's a travesty of faith, an insult to God and His love. It is the expression of a subtly hidden resentment against your Creator. When you despise His creation, you are really saying that you don't like the design or care much for the Designer. You are calling unclean what God calls clean. You are failing to realize how much God loves you.

• *What right have you to belittle or despise someone whom God has honored so highly?* "Consider the incredible love that the Father has shown us in allowing us to be called 'children of God'" (1 John 3:1, Phillips). And that's not just what we're called. It's what we are. "Oh, dear children of mine ... have you realized it? Here and now we *are* God's children" (v. 2, Phillips).

Do you think that when you consider God's son or daughter worthless or inferior, He is pleased by your so-called humility?

• *What right have you to belittle or despise someone whom God values so highly?* How much does God value you? "In human experience it is a rare thing for one man to give his life for another, even if the latter be a good man . . . Yet the proof of God's amazing love is this: that it was *while we were sinners* that Christ died for us. . . . we may hold our heads high in the light of God's love" (Romans 5:7-8, 11, Phillips). God has declared your value. You are someone whom God values so highly as to give the life of His own dear Son to redeem you.

• *What right have you to belittle or despise someone whom God has provided for so fully?* "How much more shall your Father which is in heaven give good things?" (Matthew 7:11, KJV). "God shall supply all your need" (Philippians 4:19, KJV). This doesn't sound as if He wants you to be self-loathing or to feel inadequate.

• *What right have you to belittle or despise someone whom God has planned for so carefully?*

Praise be to God . . . for giving us through Christ every spiritual benefit . . . consider what he has done—before the foundation of the world he chose us to become, in Christ, his holy and blameless children living within his constant care. He planned, in his purpose of love, that we should be adopted as his own children *(Ephesians 1:3-5, Phillips).*

• *What right have you to belittle or despise someone in whom God delights?* The apostle Paul said that we are "accepted in the beloved" (Ephesians 1:6, KJV). Do you remember the Father's words at the baptism of Jesus? "This is my beloved Son, in whom I am well pleased" (Matthew 3:17, KJV). Paul gives us a daring thought: we are "in Christ." He used this phrase some 90 times. You are in Christ, therefore you are in the Beloved. God looks at you in Christ and says to you, "You are My beloved son, you are My beloved daughter, in whom I am well pleased."

From where will you get your idea of yourself? From distortions of your childhood? From past hurts and false ideas that have been programmed into you? Or will you say, "No, I will not listen to those lies from the past any longer. I will not listen to Satan, the liar, the confuser, the blinder, who twists and distorts. I am going to listen to God's opinion of me, and let Him reprogram me until His loving estimate of me becomes a part of my life, right down to my innermost feelings."

Cooperate with the Holy Spirit

You must become a partner with God in this reprogramming and renewal process. Such work is a continuous process, not a sudden crisis. I don't know of any single Christian experience that will change your self-image overnight. You are to be "transformed by the renewing of your mind" (Romans 12:2, KJV). The verbs in this verse represent continuous action, and the word *mind* describes the way you think, the way you look at life as a daily process.

How can you cooperate with the Holy Spirit in doing this?

• Ask God to check you every time you belittle yourself. When you start doing this, you're in for a surprise. For you may find that your whole life-style is a direct or indirect put-down of yourself. Here are a few hints. What do you do when someone compliments you? Can you say, "Thank you"? "I'm glad you liked that"? "I appreciate that"? Or do you go into a long song and dance of cutting yourself down? If you have been belittling yourself, it'll tear you up for a while to stop, because you'll want to go through the whole routine. Don't do it.

I think the spiritualizing is the worst; it must be nauseating to God. Someone says, "I heard you sing today and I enjoyed your song." Then do you become very spiritual and say, "Well, it really wasn't me; it was the Lord"? Sure, it was the Lord; you are dependent on Him. But you don't need to say that every time.

• Let God love you, and let Him teach you how to love yourself and how to love others. You want love. You want God to affirm and accept you, and that's what He does. But because of wretched programming from the other sources, it is difficult to accept love. In fact, it is so hard that you may think it is more comfortable to go on the way you are.

I challenge you to enter the healing process, so that you can lift your head high as a son or a daughter of God himself.

Condensed by permission from *Healing for Damaged Emotions,* by David A. Seamands. Published by Victor Books and © 1981 by SP Publications, Wheaton, Ill.

Chapter 2

Am I Stuck with the Temperament I've Got?

by Jan Frye

Background Scripture: 1 Corinthians 12:12-31

I ADMIRE the fast, energetic person.

My husband, Hal, is fast. He gets up at 5 A.M., jogs for 30 minutes, spends time in devotions, completes his shower and breakfast, and arrives at work early enough to put in a 10-hour day that ends at 5:30 P.M. Then, after a recharge (dinner), he begins his evening activities. My, my. I stand in awe.

God made me from a different mold, however. I coax myself out of bed by 7 A.M. and am totally prepared for the day, devotions and all, by at least 11. I look at the clock in disbelief and then scurry around to begin the first job from my previous evening's list, hoping to somehow redeem the time. If someone calls, I generally chat with them awhile. Prioritizing relationships, I call it. And if one of my boys runs into the kitchen with a three-inch gash in his arm, I

calmly say, "Guess we'd better drive you to the emergency room, Honeybun." My, my. My husband stands in awe.

Twenty years ago I mistakenly begged God to fill me with great boldness. "Please, Lord, make me like the apostle Paul," I prayed. Within a few months from that time, I knew that Hal and I would be leaving the States to become missionaries to Papua New Guinea, an assignment that would last about six years. It seemed logical to me that the Lord could not possibly carry out His Great Commission through an easygoing leader like me.

God never changed me as I asked, but in those years He did teach me something remarkable about myself and about Him. He taught me that He wanted to refine and use the temperament He gave me.

We shouldn't confuse temperament with character. Character can—and should—change. In fact, I could have saved myself considerable discontent by asking God for more Christlike character traits, such as kindness, patience, loyalty, and honesty, than pleading for a change in temperament. Character refers to traits developed through personal discipline, training, and God's grace. Nobody is born with a natural tendency to traits of character.

Temperament, on the other hand, is a natural inclination from the time of birth. Temperament is what makes some of us outgoing and others quiet. Our temperaments are set in our genes and honed by our childhood and environment. And not even religion will change our temperament.

A couple of years ago a friend of mine told me, "I'm planning to ask the board of directors for a pay raise today." Since I come from a totally different temperament, I could not understand why she would even attempt something so outgoing. I would have spent years working harder than my colleagues in an effort to gain a raise. But I would never have asked for one.

As Michael Malone writes, in his book *Psychetypes*

(E. P. Dutton and Co.), there are a lot of different ways to be absolutely normal. When we think our temperament in life is the only right approach—that, for example, we all need to be quiet and submissive—we can expect a great deal of difficulty in dealing with others.

We all differ in our temperament, or basic approach to life. We're riding somewhere on a teeter-totter between being feelings-oriented and facts-oriented.

My friend Barbara tends to express feelings and emotions. She is the only woman I know who waves her hands and says, "I *love* that guy *so* much that I would give my right arm for just *one* day with him!" She's also the one who can naturally walk up to visitors at church and somehow convey to them a feeling of acceptance. Because of Barbara, visitors want to return. And if tension fills the air in any room at any time, Barbara is the first to notice. In fact, she goes to great lengths to clear any disharmony. She has what sociologists call a sanguine temperament.

Joe, however, tends to express ideas and information. He seldom expresses emotions. He's the church treasurer who throws his energy into doing his job efficiently. If the books don't balance, Joe will give up a fun evening to calculate until the figures are perfect. Nobody needs to prod Joe. He consistently prods himself to strive for the best. Joe has a phlegmatic temperament.

Barbara and Joe are neither right nor wrong in their approach to life. They're just different.

Some researchers say that birth order can influence our temperament. Lucille Forer, writing in *The Birth Order Factor* (David McKay Co.), claims that firstborn children tend to be more task-oriented, while later borns are often more relaxed and people-related.

I can see myself in the following chart. This chart lists some of the strengths and weaknesses that can accompany the four basic temperaments. Though the material is adapted from a similar listing by Tim LaHaye (*Understanding the Male Temperament,* Revell), the original source dates back to the fifth century B.C., to Hippocrates of Greece.

FOUR BASIC TEMPERAMENTS

EXTROVERTS

1. **Sanguine** (Actors, Salesmen, Speakers)	2. **Choleric** (Leaders, Producers, Builders)
Strengths	
outgoing	strong-willed
charismatic	independent
warm	productive
friendly	decisive
responsive	practical
talkative	visionary
enthusiastic	optimistic
carefree	courageous
compassionate	self-confident
generous	leader
Weaknesses	
undisciplined	unsympathetic
weak-willed	inconsiderate
restless	hostile—angry
disorganized	cruel—sarcastic
unproductive	unforgiving
undependable	self-sufficient
obnoxious—loud	domineering
egocentric	opinionated
exaggerates	proud
insecure	crafty

INTROVERTS _____

3. **Melancholy**	4. **Phlegmatic**
(Artists, Musicians, Inventors, Philosophers, Doctors)	(Diplomats, Accountants, Teachers, Technicians)

Strengths

gifted	calm
analytical	easygoing
perfectionist	likable
conscientious	diplomatic
loyal	organized
aesthetic	dependable
idealistic	conservative
sensitive	practical
self-sacrificing	reluctant leader
self-disciplined	dry humor

Weaknesses

moody	unmotivated
negative	blasé
critical	indolent
legalistic	spectator
self-centered	selfish
touchy	stingy
revengeful	stubborn
persecution-prone	self-protective
unsociable	indecisive
theoretical	fearful

When I attempt to line myself up with this diagram, I'm reminded of the scripture, "Each one should test his own actions. Then he can take pride in himself, without comparing himself to somebody else" (Galatians 6:4). We really don't have to envy the strengths of others, for just like them, we have our own set of strengths. And God can use our strengths in ways He can't use the strengths of those who have different temperaments.

Of course, no one person fits each temperament pattern perfectly. I can see that I'm strongly phlegmatic in temperament, for example, but I also exhibit some sanguine tendencies. I'm encouraged when I recognize that my reluctance to lead is quite normal and that this can actually be a strength (too many chiefs can be a problem, you know).

Believe it or not, one of my most rewarding and fruitful ministries as a missionary in Papua New Guinea came directly out of my tendency to be quiet, calm, and slow. Every week I met in my living room with the Papua New Guinean pastors' wives. I would listen to their lengthy prayer requests, and then we would all walk into my bedroom, kneel around my bed, and pray for at least two hours. Some of the more action-oriented missionaries told me this would have been difficult for them.

As I look at the chart of characteristics, it comforts me—some, at least—that stubbornness is a weakness others of my temperament grapple with. Of course I don't have to let this weakness dominate me. I know the power of the Holy Spirit can chisel off the abrasive edges of this weakness, and I can learn to better recognize my stubbornness when it surfaces, and then back off when I become too hardheaded. And I can learn to value my stubbornness when it's time to say a firm no to temptation. (Sometimes, what we consider a weakness can actually become a strength.)

Satan wants to overwhelm us with guilt for not being like others we admire. But Jesus wants to overwhelm us with thanksgiving for the way He made us. Then we can pray, "Lord, I trust You to refine and use even my stubbornness for You. I'm excited to see how You're going to work through me today."

Jan Frye is a free-lance writer of Littleton, Colo. She and her husband are a marriage enrichment leader couple in their denomination. As such, they conduct retreats and seminars for married couples.

Chapter 3

Healing Damaged Emotions

by David A. Seamands

Background Scripture: Romans 8:26-27; James 5:16

ONE SUNDAY EVENING in 1966, I preached a sermon called "The Holy Spirit and the Healing of Our Damaged Emotions." It was my first venture into this area, and I was convinced that God had given me that message, or I would never have had the courage to preach it. What I said that evening about the healing of the memories and damaged emotions is now old hat. You will find it in a lot of books. But it wasn't old then.

The Problem

Through the years, as tapes have gone out all over the world, letters and testimonies have confirmed my belief that there is another realm of problems which requires a special kind of prayer and a deeper level of healing by the Spirit. Somewhere between our sins, on the one hand, and our sick-

nesses, on the other, lies an area the Scripture calls "in-firmities."

We can explain this by an illustration from nature. If you visit the far West, you will see those beautiful giant sequoia and redwood trees. In most of the parks the natural-ists can show you a cross section of a great tree they have cut, and point out that the rings of the tree reveal the devel-opmental history, year by year. Here's a ring that represents a year when there was a terrible drought. Here are a couple of rings from years when there was too much rain. Here's where the tree was struck by lightning. All of this lies em-bedded in the heart of the tree, representing the autobiogra-phy of its growth.

And that's the way it is with us. Just a few minutes beneath the protective bark, the concealing, protective mask, are the recorded rings of our lives.

There are scars of ancient, painful hurts . . . as when a little boy rushed downstairs one Christmas dawn and dis-covered in his Christmas stocking a dirty old rock, put there to punish him for some trivial boyhood naughtiness. This scar has eaten away in him, causing all kinds of inter-personal difficulties.

Here is the discoloration of a tragic stain that muddied all of life . . . as years ago behind the barn, or in the haystack, or out in the woods, a big brother took a little sister and introduced her into the mysteries—no, the miseries of sex.

And here we see the pressure of a painful, repressed memory . . . of running after an alcoholic father who was about to kill the mother, and then of rushing for the butcher knife. Such scars have been buried in pain so long that they are causing hurt and rage that are inexplicable. And these scars are not touched by conversion and sanctifying grace, or by the ordinary benefits of prayer.

In the rings of our thoughts and emotions, the record is there; the memories are recorded, and all are alive. And they directly and deeply affect our concepts, our feelings, our re-lationships. They affect the way we look at life and God, at others and ourselves.

We preachers have often given people the mistaken idea that the new birth and being "filled with the Spirit" are going to automatically take care of these emotional hang-ups. But this just isn't true. A great crisis experience of Jesus Christ, as important and eternally valuable as this is, is not a shortcut to emotional health. It is not a quickie cure for personality problems.

Some may object: "What are you doing? Are you de-nying the power of the Holy Spirit to heal our hangups? Are you trying to give us a copout for responsibility, so that we can blame life, or heredity, or parents, or teachers, or sweet-hearts, or mates for our defeats and failures? In the words of Paul: 'Shall we continue in sin, that grace may abound?'" (Romans 6:1, KJV).

And I would answer as Paul answered that question, "God forbid!" What I am saying is that certain areas of our lives need special healing by the Holy Spirit. Because they are not subject to ordinary prayer, discipline, and willpower, they need a special kind of understanding, an unlearning of past wrong programming, and a relearning and reprogramming transformation by the renewal of our minds. And this is not done overnight by a crisis experience.

Two Extremes

Understanding these things will protect us from two extremes. Some Christians see anything that wiggles as the devil. Let me say a kind but firm word to young or immature Christians. Throughout the centuries the church has been very careful about declaring a person demon-possessed. There *is* such a thing as demon possession. On rare occasions, during my many years of ministry, I have felt led to take the authority of the name of Jesus to cast out what I have believed was an evil spirit, and I have seen deliverance and healing.

But only careful, prayerful, mature, Spirit-filled Christians should ever attempt anything in the nature of exorcism. I spend a lot of time in the counseling room, picking up the pieces of people who have been utterly disillusioned and devastated, because immature Christians tried to cast imaginary demons out of them.

The other extreme is an overly simplistic pat-answer syndrome, which says, "Read your Bible. Pray. Have more faith. If you were spiritually OK, you wouldn't have this hangup. You would never get depressed. You would never have any sexual compulsions or problems."

However, people who say such things are being cruel. They are only piling more weights on a person who is in pain and unsuccessfully struggling with an emotionally rooted problem.

Perhaps you have heard about the man who was traveling on a dinner flight. When he opened his prepackaged meal, right on top of the salad he saw an enormous roach. When he got home he wrote an indignant letter to the president of that airline. A few days later, a special delivery letter came from the president. He was all apologies. "This was very unusual, but don't worry. I want to assure you that that particular airplane has been completely fumigated. In fact, all the seats and the upholstery have been stripped out. We have taken disciplinary action against the stewardess who served you that meal, and she may even be fired. It is highly probable that this particular aircraft will be taken out of service. I can assure you that it will never happen again. And I trust you will continue to fly with us."

Well, the man was terrifically impressed by such a letter, until he noticed something. Quite by accident the letter he had written had stuck to the back of the president's letter. When he looked at his own letter, he saw a note at the bottom that said, "Reply with the regular roach letter."

So often we reply with the regular roach letter to people suffering with emotional problems. We give pat, over-simplified answers, which drive them to deeper despair and disillusionment.

The Evidence

What are some of these damaged emotions? One of the most common is a deep *sense of unworthiness,* a continuous feeling of anxiety, inadequacy, and inferiority, an inner nagging that says, "I'm no good. I'll never amount to anything. No one could ever possibly love me. Everything I do is wrong."

What happens to this kind of person, when he becomes a Christian? Part of his mind believes in God's love, accepts God's forgiveness, and feels at peace for a while. Then, all of a sudden, everything within him rises up to cry out, "It's a lie! Don't believe it! Don't pray! There's no one up there to hear you. No one really cares. There's no one to relieve your anxiety. How could God possibly love you and forgive some-one like you? You're too bad!"

What has happened? The good news of the gospel has not penetrated down into his damaged inner self, which also needs to be evangelized. His deep inner scars must be touched and healed by the Balm of Gilead.

Then there's another kind, that for want of a better term, I call the *perfectionist complex.* This is the inner feeling that says, "I can never quite achieve. I never do anything well enough. I can't please myself, others, or God." This kind of a person is always groping, striving, usually feeling guilty, driven by inner oughts and shoulds. "I ought to be able to do this. I should be able to do that. I must be a little bit better." He's ever climbing, but never reaching.

What happens to this person, when he becomes a Christian? Tragically enough, he usually transfers his perfectionism onto his relationship with God, who is seen now as a figure on top of a tall ladder. He says to himself, "I'm going to climb up to God now. I'm His child, and I want to please Him, more than I want anything else."

So he starts climbing, rung by rung, working so hard, until his knuckles are bleeding and his shins are bruised. Finally, he reaches the top, only to find that his God has moved up three rungs.

Some years ago I received a telephone call from the wife of a minister friend of mine, asking me to counsel her husband who had just suffered a complete nervous breakdown. As we were driving to the hospital, she began to talk about him. "I just don't understand Bill. It's almost as if he has a built-in slave driver that won't let him go. His people just love him; and they would do anything for him, but he can't let them."

I began to visit with Bill, and after he was well enough to talk, he told me about his home and his childhood. As Bill grew up he wanted very much to please his parents. He tried to win his mother's approval by occasionally helping her set the table. But she'd say, "Bill, you've got the knives in the wrong place." So he would put the knives in the right place. "Now you've got the forks wrong." After that it would be the salad plates. He could never please her.

Try as hard as he might, he could never please his father either. He brought him his report card with B's and C's. His dad looked at the card and said, "Bill, I think if you try, you could surely get all B's, couldn't you?" So he studied harder and harder, until one day he brought home all B's. Dad said, "But surely, you know, if you just put a little more effort into it, you could get all A's." So he worked and struggled through a semester or two, until finally he got all A's. He was so excited—now Mother and Dad would surely be pleased with him. He ran home, for he could hardly wait. Dad looked at the report card and said, "Well, I know those teachers. They always give A's."

When Bill became a minister, all he did was exchange one mother and one father for several hundred of them: his congregation became his unpleasable parents. He could never satisfy them, no matter what he did. Finally, he just collapsed under the sheer weight of struggling for approval and trying to prove himself.

Then there is another kind of damaged emotion that we can call *supersensitivity*. The supersensitive person has usually been hurt deeply. He reached out for love and approval and affection, but instead he got the opposite, and he has scars deep inside of him. Sometimes he sees things other people don't see, and tends to feel things other people don't feel.

One day I was walking down the street and saw supersensitive Charlie coming toward me. I usually give him a lot of attention, but that morning I was very busy so I just said, "Hi, Charlie. How are you?" and passed on by. When I got back to the office, a church member called me on the phone and asked, "Are you mad at Charlie?"

"Charlie who?"

"Well, you know, Charlie Olson."

"Why, no. I just saw him down the street." Then I suddenly realized that I hadn't given Charlie the appreciation and the affirmation I usually do, knowing he is supersensitive.

Supersensitive people need a lot of approval. You can never quite give them enough. And sometimes they seem very insensitive. They have been hurt so badly that instead of becoming sensitive, they cover it by being hard, tough. They want to get even and hurt others. So quite unbeknown to them, they spend their lives pushing people around, hurting and dominating them. They use money or authority or position or sex or even sermons to hurt people. Does all this affect their Christian experience? Yes, very deeply.

Then there are the people who are filled with *fears.* Perhaps the greatest of them all is the fear of failure.

I remember some years ago talking with a salesman in a used car lot. As we looked out the showroom window, we saw a man who was going around kicking tires on the cars. He was also raising the hoods and banging the fenders. The salesman said disgustedly, "Look at that guy out there. He's a wheel-kicker. They are the bane of our existence. They come in here all the time, but never buy cars because they can't make up their minds. Now watch him out there. He's kicking the tires. He'll say the wheels are out of line. He'll listen to the motor and say, 'Hear that knock?' Nobody else can hear the knock, but he can hear it. Something is always wrong. He is afraid to choose; but he can never make up his mind, so he always finds an excuse."

Life is filled with wheel-kickers, people who fear failure, fear making the wrong decision. What happens to such people as they approach the Christian life? Believing is a great risk; it's very hard. Decisions tear them up. Faith comes hard. Witnessing is difficult. Launching out in the Holy Spirit and really surrendering to God is almost a trauma. Discipline is difficult. The fearful people live on *if onlys:* "If only this or if only that, then I would be OK." But since the *if only* never comes to pass, they usually never accomplish what they would like to. The fearful are the defeated and the indecisive.

The whole area of *sex* is intricately mixed in with all these others, but needs a special word said about it.

In our society, it is very difficult for anyone to grow to young adulthood without suffering some damage in the sex department of his personality.

I'm thinking of scores of people who have come to me for help. I remember a lady who had heard me speak in her church and then drove 1,200 miles to talk with me. I remember a man who finally came into the office and said that he had driven 11 times around the church, getting up enough nerve to come and see me. Both of these people were genuine Christians, and both were struggling with problems of homosexuality.

I am thinking of a young lady in a distant university where I held a preaching mission. To this day I don't know what she looks like, for she kept her back turned to me and her coat pulled up around her face, as she sat in a corner, sobbing. Finally, she said, "I've got to share this with someone before I explode." Then, still facing the corner, she told me the sad story which we hear more and more often these days, about a father who had treated her not as a daughter, but as a wife.

I am thinking of scores of young men and women who were fed a lot of false and harmful ideas by well-meaning but ignorant parents and preachers. Now they are unfit for marriage, unable to be husbands and wives who can live without fear, guilt, and shame. Damaged? Yes, badly damaged.

Does the gospel have a message for these various kinds of emotionally damaged persons? For if it doesn't offer healing for all of them, then we had better put a padlock on our church doors, quit playing Christianity, and shut up about our "good news."

Divine Repairs

Does God have some repairs for us? Yes, He does! Paul wrote to the Roman Christians about the Holy Spirit who *helps our infirmities* (see Romans 8:26, KJV). Many of the modern translations use *weaknesses* or *cripplings* in place of

the word *infirmities.* One meaning of the word *help* has a
medical connotation, suggesting the way a nurse helps in the
healing process. So it is not simply "to take hold of on the
other side," which is the literal meaning of the verb, but that
the Holy Spirit becomes our Partner and Helper, who works
along with us in a mutual participation, for our healing.

What is our part in the healing of our damaged emotions? The Holy Spirit is, indeed, the divine Counselor, the
divine Psychiatrist, who gets ahold of our problem on the
other end. But we're on this end of it. Just what are you and
I supposed to do in this healing process?

1. Face your problem squarely. With ruthless moral
honesty, and with God's grace, confront that awful, hidden
childhood memory, however deep the feelings within you.
Acknowledge it to yourself, and acknowledge it to another
human being. Some problems can never be solved until you
confess them to others. "Confess your faults one to another,
and pray one for another, that you may be healed" (James
5:16, KJV). Some people miss deep inner healing because
they lack the courage to share deeply with another person.

2. Accept your responsibility in the matter. "But," you
say, "I was sinned against. I was a victim. You don't know
what happened to me."

True enough. But what about your response? What
about the fact that you learned to hate or resent, or to escape
into an unreal world?

You may say, "My folks never told me anything about
sex, and I grew up and I went out into this evil world, innocent and ignorant, and got into trouble." That's the way it
happened the first time. But what about the second time or
the third time—whose fault was it then? Life is like a com-
plicated tapestry, woven with a loom and shuttle. Heredity,
environment, all the things experienced in childhood, from
parents, teachers, playmates, all of life's handicaps—all of
these things are on one side of the loom, and they pass the
shuttle to you. But remember, you pass the shuttle back

through the loom. And this action, together with your responses, weaves the design in the tapestry of your life. You are responsible for your actions. You will never receive healing for your damaged emotions until you stop blaming everyone else and accept your responsibility.

3. *Ask yourself if you want to be healed.* This is what Jesus asked the sick man who had lain ill for 38 years (John 5:6). Do you really want to be healed, or do you just want to talk about your problem? Do you want to use your problem to get sympathy from others? Do you just want it for a crutch, so that you can walk with a limp?

The lame man said to Jesus, "But, Lord, nobody puts me into the pool. I try, but they all get there ahead of me." It seems as though he would not look deep within his heart to find out whether he really wanted to be healed.

4. *Forgive everyone who is involved in your problem.* Facing responsibility and forgiving people are really two sides of the same coin. The reason some people have never been able to forgive is that if they forgave, the last rug would be pulled out from under them and they would have no one to blame. Facing responsibility and forgiving are almost the same action; in some instances you need to do them simultaneously. Jesus made it very plain that no healing occurs until there is deep forgiveness.

5. *Forgive yourself.* So many Christians say, "Yes, I know that God has forgiven me, but I can never forgive myself." This statement is a contradiction in terms. How can you really believe that God has forgiven you, and then not forgive yourself? When God forgives, He buries your sins in the sea of His forgiveness and His forgetfulness. As Corrie ten Boom says, "He then puts a sign on the bank which says: 'No fishing allowed.'" You have no right to dredge up anything that God has forgiven and forgotten. He has put it behind His back. Through an inscrutable mystery, divine omniscience has somehow forgotten your sins. You *can* forgive yourself.

6. Ask the Holy Spirit to show you what your real problem is, and how you need to pray. Paul said that often we do not know how to pray as we ought (Romans 8:26). But the Holy Spirit prays in and through us, and makes intercession for us. Sometimes the Holy Spirit uses a temporary assistant in the form of a human counselor, who can help us to perceive what the real problem is. Sometimes the Spirit is able to do this through God's Word or through some incident in life that suddenly makes us aware of our real problem.

Do you remember the story of Henry Ford and Charlie Steinmetz? Steinmetz was a dwarf, ugly and deformed, but he had one of the greatest minds in the field of electricity that the world has ever known. Steinmetz built the great generators for Henry Ford in his first plant in Dearborn, Mich. One day those generators broke down and the plant came to a halt. They brought in ordinary mechanics and helpers who couldn't get the generators going again. They were losing money. Then Ford called Steinmetz. The genius came, seemed to just putter around for a few hours, and then threw the switch that put the great Ford plant back into operation.

A few days later Henry Ford received a bill from Steinmetz for $10,000. Although Ford was a very rich man, he returned the bill with a note, "Charlie, isn't this bill just a little high for a few hours of tinkering around on those motors?"

Steinmetz returned the bill to Ford. This time it read: "For tinkering around on the motors: $10. For knowing where to tinker: $9,990. Total: $10,000." Henry Ford paid the bill.

The Holy Spirit knows where to tinker. We do not know what we ought to be praying for. We often do not receive, because we ask for the wrong things. As you read these chapters, ask the Holy Spirit to show you what you need to know about yourself, and then to guide you in your prayers.

Condensed by permission from *Healing for Damaged Emotions*, by David A. Seamands. Published by Victor Books and © 1981 by SP Publications, Wheaton, Ill.

Chapter 4

When Fear Envelops You

by Erwin Lutzer

Background Scripture: Matthew 14:22-31

HAVE YOU EVER HEARD someone make one of the following statements?

"I'll never drive a car in Chicago. Never! That kind of traffic scares me to death."

"Don't ever ask me to say something in public. I'd be so scared that I would forget everything I wanted to say."

Or consider what a woman told me last week: "Because of a past relationship with a man, I've lived in fear for five years, afraid he'll come to the door or kill me when I go outside. So I lock myself upstairs when I'm home alone."

Fear. The kind of fear that can paralyze, that can prevent you from enjoying life, that can lock up deep inside the gifts that God has given you, never to be used.

Some fears are normal and actually for our benefit. This kind of fear motivates you to take the children into the basement of your house when you hear that a tornado may be coming. It causes you to warn your children about the danger of playing with matches and the danger of stopping to talk to strangers.

There is a third kind of fear, a fear for which there is no logical reason. Irrational fear makes no sense to the onlooker—and usually doesn't make sense to the one afraid, either. Some people, for example, are afraid of crowds. They are fine one-on-one, but as soon as a group gathers in their area, they start to feel uncomfortable. When you ask them why they are afraid of a crowd, they cannot explain it.

Some people are afraid of marriage. Others are afraid they will lose their jobs and live with their fear year in and year out. You may be one of those afraid to go home because you keep wondering what might have happened in your absence.

"I misjudged you, Osgood. At first I thought you were a mover and a shaker. Now I see you were just trembling."

Whatever your fear, the first thing you need to remember is that God created you with the capacity to fear. He built that emotional response within you just as surely as He gave you the ability to love and respond warmly to other people. Fear is part of His loving provision for us. Properly controlled, fear can protect us from harm, and it can motivate us to positive action. Uncontrolled fear, however, can put us into a personal prison and stunt our personal and spiritual growth.

This chapter is designed to help you understand and control your fear. I want to help you push back the walls of the prison that fear has built for you so that you can go free.

At this point you may be saying, "I don't really want to do that. I built that wall myself to protect me from hurt. I laid a very careful and deep foundation. I built the walls sky high and am determined to live behind those walls."

You may be like some people I know. They are afraid to have company in their home. For 25 years they've lived in their lovely home and never invited anyone over, not even for coffee. They are afraid the water might not boil, that the cake won't turn out right, that their company won't like their living room decor. Something is bound to go wrong if they ever open that front door to others. These fears are the walls they won't push aside. In fact, their fears have become their security blanket that they hug to their bosom as tightly as Linus carries his blanket.

The apostle Paul has a message for you. He wrote to Timothy, "For God hath not given us the spirit of fear" (2 Timothy 1:7, KJV). And the apostle John reminded us that "perfect love casts out fear" (1 John 4:18, NASB). You can be free from the bondage of fear. Fear need not control your actions.

The paralyzing effect of fear is illustrated by one of the incidents in Jesus' life, related in Matthew 14:22-31. Jesus had just fed the 5,000 men, plus women and children. The crowd was thinning out when He asked the disciples to get into a boat and head for the other side of the lake, where He would meet them. He went up into the mountain to pray.

When the boat was about four miles from shore, a storm sprang up. The wind buffeted the little boat, and the waves began pounding against the side of it. Inasmuch as many of the disciples were fishermen, this was no new experience even though it was very dangerous, but what they saw coming across the water was definitely not normal. Walking toward them *on the water* was the figure of a man. The Scriptures record: "And when the disciples saw Him walking on the sea, they were frightened, saying, 'It is a ghost!' And they cried out for fear" (v. 26, NASB). Sound like a tough group of fishermen?

The experience of these disciples points to the first step in demolishing the walls of fear—**you must see your fear in perspective.** Matthew reported that Jesus came to those disciples, and they thought that He was a ghost. They had a fear of the storm based on experience, but their greater fear came from perceiving Jesus' figure as a ghost.

That reaction is not unusual even today. There are many who believe that when a person dies, his spirit might return to traverse the earth, haunting different places and people. You and I know this is not true; yes, there are spirits that do haunt certain people and places, but those are not human spirits. They are evil, demonic spirits. The disciples were not that spiritually perceptive yet, so when their superstitious minds focused on the advancing figure, they naturally assumed it was a ghost. They could not relate this experience to anything that had ever happened to them before, as they had never seen anyone walk on water. Only after the initial outcry caused by fear did anyone even dream that it was Jesus who was the object of their fear.

What can you learn from this about your perspective on fear? You must see that **Jesus is in the midst of your fear.** Fear has a way of distorting our perception, and we don't see and understand the true object of our fears, but wrapped up in that object are the loving arms and concern of Jesus Christ.

Dr. Harry Ironside used to tell a story about himself that also illustrates this point. He would pretend that he was a bear. He would get on his hands and knees and chase his son around the room, all the while growling like a bear. The little boy would become fearful and be really frightened at first. Then one day when the little boy was backed into a corner, he suddenly turned and rushed into his father's arms. "You're not a bear, you're my papa!" he said.

From that incident, Dr. Ironside learned an important lesson: Often the experience we fear the most is actually an act of God. He is attempting to put His arms around us. That's why I can say with full assurance that Jesus is in the midst of your fear. The misinterpretation, the misunderstanding, that has come to you as a result of that fear can be dissipated, when you realize that Jesus Christ is in the midst of it—just as He was in the midst of the disciples' fear.

There is something else you must understand if you are to get the proper perspective on your fear. Not only is Jesus Christ in the midst of your fear, but **Jesus also knows what your fear is all about and the feelings it gives you.**

When Jesus came to the disciples during the fourth watch at night, He said to them, "Take courage, it is I; do not be afraid" (v. 27, NASB). I particularly like the line in the first part of the verse: "But immediately Jesus spoke to them." He recognized their fear and immediately set about allaying it.

What had tipped off Jesus that the disciples were afraid? Had He overheard their cry of fear? No, I'm convinced that He knew it because He is the Son of God, and He knew what was troubling their hearts. There just was no way their voices could have reached Him during the high wind.

As you read this, what fear is uppermost in your mind? What is the fear that possibly keeps you awake for part of the night, that limits your effectiveness on the job, that hampers your service for Christ? Name it—and then know that Jesus knew all along that it was there in your heart and occupying your mind.

God knew all about the fear that would consume you when He inserted the message "Fear not" more than 100 times in the Bible. You ask, "Why 100 times? Wouldn't once be enough?" Those of you who are parents of preschool children probably know why. My wife and I, at least, have had to tell our children some things at least 100 times! Why? Because my wife and I have learned that sometimes even 99 times are not enough. And God said "Fear not" over 100 times because He knows what is going on inside you, and He knows that when we are paralyzed by fear we don't hear very well.

Before we go on to the second step in overcoming our fears, let's summarize the first: To deal with fear, you must get a proper perspective on your fear, and that happens only when you recognize that Jesus is in the midst of it and knows all about your fear. This then leads us to the second step— **you must have the right focus during your fear if you are to get help.**

Let's examine Peter's experience with Christ. Jesus said as He approached the boat, "It is I." To this Peter quickly responded, "Lord, if it is You, command me to come to You on the water" (v. 28, NASB). He was ready for a quick test of the authenticity of that voice and Person.

Some people are like that. They are never sure whether God means what He says, and they always want to test it out. That can be dangerous, for the Bible says, "You shall not put the Lord your God to the test" (Deuteronomy 6:16, NASB). Yet in this instance, Peter did risk the test and say, "If it is You"—implying that he wasn't quite sure yet—"command me to come to You on the water."

Jesus said, "Come!"

When Peter began walking on the water, he was on solid

ground with the Lord. The Bible says he "came toward Jesus," implying his eyes were on Jesus (v. 29, NASB). When his eyes shifted focus and saw the waves, he didn't see only the waves but also the wind that was so boisterous. At that moment, "he became afraid" and began to sink (v. 30, NASB).

Like a lot of us, Peter had within him the alternating spirits of fear and trust. When he looked at the Lord, he trusted. When he looked at the circumstances in which he was with the Lord, he became afraid.

Instead of focusing on the circumstances, your focus must be on the promises of God. Jesus had in effect promised Peter that he would be able to walk on the water and make it all the way to Jesus. Peter should have focused on that promise and kept walking, regardless of the activity of the wind and waves. He did not do it and started sinking as fear of the wind took hold in his heart.

Focusing on the promises of God means that we are obedient to the call of God in them. We choose to obey despite the fears that might arise from circumstances. Let's suppose your problem is fear of crowds. You simply feel uncomfortable as soon as more than half a dozen people are gathered together. Let's further suppose you are paralyzed by that fear. Determined to overcome that fear, no matter what, you decide to go into that crowd, saying inside yourself, "I will overcome this fear, I will overcome this fear." Do you think fear will flee as the crowd begins engulfing you?

Certainly not, because your whole focus is on your fear, and the minute you get into that crowd, that fear will again come upon you. It will arise like the mist at dawn and envelop your heart, and you'll rush out of that crowd, totally defeated.

On the other hand, your focus can be on obedience. You can say to yourself, "God in His Word has commanded me to get together with His people, and this fear is hindering me from doing that. So I will focus on Him. If I happen to become afraid in a crowd, and I'm hoping I won't, I will simply have to live with it. I will accept it because it has happened before and I have lived through it. Thus I will be obedient regardless of my feelings of fear." If you do that, you will soon discover that your attention will shift away from your fears. Soon you will be able to be in crowds, preoccupied with your responsibility to interact with others and love them as Christ commanded. In time, those fears will not trouble you anymore.

The reason for this is both psychological and spiritual. The psychological reason is that when we focus on the very thing we are trying to be rid of, its power over us actually increases. In this case, fear becomes a self-fulfilling prophecy. If you focus on how afraid you are, you will soon discover that you are very much afraid—indeed, your fear will grow stronger. But if your focus is on Jesus and on your obedience to Him, His power will flow through your whole being and help drive away the fear.

If Peter had kept his eyes on Jesus, he would have been able to walk across the Atlantic Ocean as long as Jesus had said, "Come." The Bible teaches that perfect love casts out fear, and the reason it does is that your love for God and His promises transcends the fear and overcomes that crippling force in your spiritual life.

Consider the woman who is afraid of dogs. One day when she hears a dog snarl, she remembers that her one-year-old son is outside playing. Without a doubt she will rush outside, grab the child, and run back inside even if the dog comes at her. Her love is stronger than her fear. How much more is loving obedience to God able to overcome paralyzing fear!

I truly feel sorry for people who live in a constant state of fear. They are forever taking their spiritual temperature to see how much fear they happen to have today. Their focus on their fear only increases it. Throw away the thermometer and begin basking in the glow of God's warm love, for it will cast out fear.

Yet the experience of Peter and the disciples that night reminds us of another step in overcoming fear. To be truly victorious over fear, you need not only a proper perspective on your fear and proper focus in your fear, but **you also need a proper faith.**

Notice what Jesus did when Peter cried out in his fear, "Lord, save me!" He stretched out His hand and took hold of Peter before he had gone down very far. Then He said, "O you of little faith, why did you doubt?" (v. 31, NASB). He pointedly referred to the real reason for Peter's failure, his lack of faith in Jesus Christ.

Let me remind you of three things that are involved in proper faith. First, you must recognize that God can ordain fearful circumstances. "Hold it," you're saying, "run that by me again." OK, why were the disciples in the boat in the middle of a dangerous storm at the fourth watch of the night? **They were there because Jesus had told them to get into the boat and cross the lake ahead of Him.** They received explicit instructions and obeyed Him implicitly, yet despite that they found themselves in the middle of a storm.

As lovingly as I can, let me remind you that sometimes the most holy path is the roughest path. Some of you are probably saying, "That's true. I gave up my job for Jesus Christ. I could be earning more money, but I believe God has called me into a ministry for Him. So now we are making less money and are starting to have problems in our family. We are experiencing health problems on top of everything, even though we believe we obeyed God." That was exactly the experience of Jesus' disciples—circumstances were difficult even though they were doing the will of God!

But God not only ordains some fearful circumstances; we can be grateful that He also monitors all of them—that is, He keeps close watch on how we are faring in the midst of the storms of life. Although the disciples couldn't see Christ when the storm began, He could see them! Isn't that true of our experience? Often we wonder where Christ is or whether He has lost interest in our predicament, but He is on the sidelines, watching the whole ordeal. And when push comes to shove as it so often does in life, I would prefer that Christ see me rather than that I see Him!

Christ carefully monitored the situation and came to them in their distress. He calculated the best time to come to them personally. It happened to be 3 a.m., the darkest hour of the night. No sooner nor any later did Christ choose to make His appearance. The disciples, exhausted by the storm and frustrated by Christ's apparent indifference to their plight, had come to the end of their rope—Christ met them there (and calmed the storm [v. 32], even though His appearance was initially more frightening than the storm).

Where are you in your battle with fear? Is the evening turning to darkness, or is the darkness already beginning to blend into the morning light? Wherever, I want you to remember that Christ is near, taking inventory of your situation and available when you turn to Him. His timing is perfect, His love intense. The Psalmist wrote, "I sought the Lord, and he answered me; he delivered me from all my fears" (Psalm 34:4). Like the disciples, this man came to worship the God who delivered him from his fears.

Let me be clear: Learning to focus on God's promises in faith does not mean that God will always change the fearful circumstances. Sometimes the storms of life continue; often those fearful situations rear their ugly heads once again. But though the circumstances might not change, we will. We will live without those paralyzing fears that rob us of our Christian freedom.

Finally, in the Scriptures there is a direct connection between God's presence and the absence of fear. For example, Hebrews 13:5-6 implies that we can be free from the fear of poverty and the fear of men by remembering that God is with us: "Let your character be free from the love of money, being content with what you have; for He Himself has said, 'I will never desert you, nor will I ever forsake you,' so that we confidently say, 'The Lord is my helper, I will not be afraid. What shall man do to me?'" (NASB). We can be content with our possessions and free from the fear of men because God will never abandon us. We've always got Him beside us.

The circumstances that we fear remind me of the walls in a penitentiary in British Columbia. When the structure was being demolished, the workmen discovered something interesting. Though the gates were steel and the windows were barred, the outer walls were made only of woodboard covered with clay and paper, painted to look as if the walls were thick metal. Anyone could have gone through those walls with little effort, but no prisoner ever tried it—they all believed the walls could never budge.

You will find that your fears are much the same; the walls you have built may appear formidable. You may even feel comfortable in your prison and find the thought of freedom frightening.

But today, you can push down those walls in the name of Jesus Christ. In your fears you can see the face of Jesus Christ disguised; you can choose to memorize God's promises rather than catering to your fluctuating emotions. You can accept the storms of life as God's will, His plan for strengthening your faith. You can join Peter in stepping out of the boat and walking with Christ. The circumstances that threaten to be over your head will suddenly be under your feet!

You'll have the exhilaration of stepping onto a cloud and discovering that your feet are on solid rock. Christ has already conquered your fears. Are you ready to accept His victory?

Condensed by permission from *Managing Your Emotions,* by Erwin Lutzer. Published by Victor Books and © 1983 by SP Publications, Wheaton, Ill.

Chapter 5

Alone Again

by Craig Selness

Background Scripture: Jeremiah 20:7-18

For SOME REASON my loneliest moments have always involved snow. Maybe that is because I grew up in Minnesota, and so many moments of any kind involved snow.

As an adolescent I was basically a loner. My favorite social activity was walking my dog. I especially enjoyed taking Toby out in the winter, when the drifts of snow were so deep that Toby's walking consisted of jumping from one footprint to another, as I blazed a trail through the backyard and up the hill overlooking our house. Yet as I stood in the quiet under the large misshapen tree that crowned the hill we had just climbed, I could not help but be struck with a twinge of loneliness when I realized that my most intimate companion was the furry creature that lay panting and shivering at my feet.

When It Hurts to Be Alone

Loneliness belongs to all of us. It is not the exclusive domain of the person who lives alone or the traveling salesperson. Loneliness is common property.

Some have even named loneliness the number-one problem in America. Dr. Billy Graham called it the most pervasive problem he has encountered. Dr. Carin Ruben-stein, a social psychologist at New York University, asserts that more than a quarter of all Americans, over 50 million people, are "painfully lonely." A survey of 40,000 readers of *Psychology Today* revealed that 67 percent of all men and women often feel lonely. Dr. James Lynch, scientific director of psychosomatic clinics at the University of Maryland School of Medicine, declares,

> Loneliness is the major contributor to disease—mental and physical—in our society. The statistics are awesome. It cuts across all ages. Loneliness is a very depressive condition, and if it is serious enough, people who are lonely will destroy themselves.[1]

Loneliness can also drive people to compromise their own moral standards. For such people, anything is better than the continuing agony of being alone. A church in southern California took a survey of their singles' group and discovered that out of 203 people, only 45 had managed to resist the temptation of immorality. When asked to list their reasons for having sexual relations despite their convictions against it, these 158 unmarried Christians listed loneliness as the overwhelming single reason.[2]

What is loneliness? Gary Collins, author of *How to Be a People-Helper,* defines it as "the painful awareness that we lack meaningful contact with others."[3]

Bill Moulder distinguishes between loneliness and solitude. Solitude is a positive time of refreshment and renewal. Loneliness is the painful experience of wanting to be with others but being unable to. Moulder describes loneliness in this way:

> What does it feel like to be lonely? I think the word that best describes the experience for me is *empty*. It feels as if there were a big hole right in the middle of my chest. Sometimes it is a dull pain, a listlessness. Even that which I enjoy most—a walk in the woods, a Bruckner symphony—seems pointless, even painful because I respond to it by

wanting to share it, and when I reach out to share it there is no one there.[4]

Some of us are driven by loneliness to do things we otherwise would not do—to drink compulsively, to eat compulsively, or to work compulsively. Some of us do nothing. For we have simply learned to accept loneliness as a way of life.

But there is hope. While loneliness is a painful and very prevalent ailment, it is not incurable. God can enable us to turn any frustration into a fulfilling experience. The frustration of loneliness is no exception.

Jeremiah, the Lonely Prophet

Before examining God's "scratch" for my itch and yours, let us see how He scratched the itch of the man who was probably the loneliest person in the Bible, the Prophet Jeremiah.

What had happened was this. Sometime after the glorious years of Israel under King David and his son, Solomon, the nation of Israel split into a Northern Kingdom, Israel, and a Southern Kingdom, Judah. Israel lasted until the year 722 B.C. when it was crushed by Assyria. Jeremiah lived about 100 years later in the nation of Judah, the Southern Kingdom.

Now the people of Judah felt quite smug about the fact that they had outlasted Israel, and were very confident that they would never be defeated, even though they were presently under a good deal of pressure from Egypt and Babylon. Their prophets assured them that they could never fall because the Temple of the Lord was in Jerusalem and surely God would not allow a heathen nation to destroy the Temple!

Then along came Jeremiah with quite a different message. For God instructed Jeremiah to tell the people of Judah that time was running out on them, that He had had enough of their deceitfulness and their pride, and was about to judge them just as He had judged Israel 100 years before.

Can you visualize Jeremiah's position? He was the only person predicting that Judah would be defeated by Babylon. He sounded like a traitor. Even worse, Jeremiah was considered a heretic. The other prophets had plenty of support for their insistence on the unassailable security of the Temple.

The people did not respond well to Jeremiah. They threw him in jail. They put him in the stocks. They tossed him into a well. On more than one occasion, they tried to kill him. Not once in the 50 years that he prophesied did the masses of Judah ever believe him.

Jeremiah was rejected, ignored, scorned, abused, hated, alone, and very lonely. He knew well the agony of loneliness. He remembered too that God had told him at the outset of his career that all of the people would turn on him (Jeremiah 1:18-19). He remembered how God had forbidden him from getting married (16:1-4). How did Jeremiah respond? His reaction was the same as many of us have had at one time or another—he got angry with God. Listen to Jeremiah's exclamation:

> O Lord, thou hast deceived me,
>   and I was deceived;
> thou art stronger than I,
>   and thou hast prevailed.
> I have become a laughingstock all the day;
>   every one mocks me. . . .
> Cursed be the day
>   on which I was born!
> The day when my mother bore me,
>   let it not be blessed! . . .
> Why did I come forth from the womb
>   to see toil and sorrow,
>   and spend my days in shame?
>   *(Jeremiah 20:7, 14, 18, RSV)*

Have you ever felt so bad that you did not think the hurt would ever go away, that you wished you had never been born? Have you ever felt deceived or cheated by God? Perhaps you have felt those pangs of hurt but have never expressed them before, even to yourself, because you were afraid you might make God angry at you or might be committing the unpardonable sin. How grateful I am to Jeremiah for having the courage to say what he felt, so that I could know that someone else has hurt as badly as I have! If you are feeling lonely or confused, tell God! He loves you and is anxious to show you His love, but often He waits to act until you cry out to Him in your need and despair.

Notice how God responded to Jeremiah's anguished accusations: "If you return, I will restore you, and you shall stand before me" (Jeremiah 15:19, RSV). God's word to Jeremiah was not one of anger or rebuke. It was a word of comfort and assurance: "Come back to Me, Jeremiah, and I will give you new energy and new hope and new life."

Is God Enough?

But is God enough? Is it fair to tell the person suffering from severe loneliness, "Trust in the Lord and let Him be your Friend"?

To answer that question, it is helpful to briefly consider the causes of loneliness. Each person has individual needs. Not everyone battles with loneliness, and not all lonely persons are lonely for the same reason.

There are many reasons why a person may be lonely. A common reason is the loss of a person very near, through death, changing locations, or breaking off a relationship. This is the loneliness of the widow, of the divorced person, of the 16-year-old boy who just lost his girlfriend to a rival.

There is a loneliness caused by developmental factors. This is the chronic feeling of loneliness experienced by the person whose parents failed early in his life to establish in him a healthy sense of worth. Such a person may never have had the confidence necessary to make new friends.

There is the loneliness of making a transition alone: going away to school for the first time, moving to a new town, beginning a new job, or battling a disease. There is the loneliness that is intensified by our affluent technological society. We think we no longer need other people to meet our needs or to entertain us. We have televisions, stereos, microwaves, and computer banking. We live in a society that cherishes independence, individualism, and competition instead of mutuality and community.

There is the loneliness of being cut off from God and alone in the universe. It is a pervading sense of fear and anger and often accompanies the contemplation of one's own death.

The underlying cause of loneliness, in summary, is the frustration of our basic human needs. As humans we have three essential needs. *First, we have a need for a relationship with God, our Creator. Second, we have a need to love and be loved.* God created us as social creatures, and in order for us to be fulfilled we need to be involved in an intimate, personal way with other people. *The third need we have is to be worthwhile to ourselves and to others.* We need to have a purpose to our lives, something to give us the sense that existence is meaningful and significant. If any of these three needs is unsatisfied, we will probably experience feelings of loneliness.

Some years ago, I did a research study on housewives, trying to find out what they actually felt about their role. After interviewing quite a number of housewives, I learned that they were basically very happy and fulfilled in their role. But I also learned that two factors caused problems. One problem arose when the husband did not give the wife the love, affection, and help that she needed. In that case her basic need for love was being frustrated. Another problem arose when the housewife began to feel that her job was basically worthless, that she as an individual was insignificant. In that case her basic need for worth was being frustrated.

What was the most fascinating to me, however, was that

in either case the feeling reported by the woman was that of loneliness! In other words, lack of people and affection in one's life is not the only cause of loneliness. A person who sits in a rest home surrounded by more people than he needs, and who gets all sorts of attention from nurses and from his family who visit him every weekend, will still feel lonesome because he thinks he has nothing to contribute. My grandfather's complaint while he lived in a nursing home was not a lack of people. After 65 years as a pastor, he felt lonely because he was now unable to do anything he considered worthwhile.

For many of us who are lonely, it is not enough to know that God is our Friend, as comforting as that is. We also have a need for meaningful relationships and a sense of worth. To cure loneliness, all three of those needs must be met.

Curing Our Loneliness

How do we go about curing our loneliness? Sometimes we learn to almost enjoy our self-pity and pain and are unwilling to do anything to change our situation. But if we are seriously interested in doing something about our hurt, there are three steps we can take.

• The first step relates to our human need to love and be loved. Most of us who feel lonely fall into the trap of waiting for someone to call or write or visit us. But this is the wrong approach. Don't wait for someone to give you. *Give first! Reach out.* Be a servant.

While I was working at a small church in Alberta, I wrestled with the dilemma of how to give adequate time to the lonely people who belonged to our church. Ours was an old church with a number of elderly and shut-in members. The solution we devised was to transport the lonely people to the rest homes in the community once every week, to visit the lonely people there. The results were outstanding! Not only were the occupants of the rest homes delighted that someone cared enough to come see them, but the people doing the visiting felt terrific. When they reached out to people in need, God gave back to them. Take the initiative—be a friend.

• The second step relates to our need for a sense of worth and meaning. The Christian needs to continually remind himself that even though he may *feel* worthless, he is not. God considers us precious (Isaiah 43:4). He was willing to die for us. We have worth simply because God created us and because we belong to Him.

If we still feel worthless even after we have reminded ourselves that we are not, we should do something about it. We can set some goals for ourselves, we can get involved in meaningful projects through our church or community. We can use our hands and build something. No matter who we are or what situation we are in, we still have the capacity to do something productive.

Vernon Anderson was a pastor and a missionary to Brazil for many years, until multiple sclerosis advanced to the point that he could no longer be active. For almost a decade Vernon has been confined to a wheelchair and a bed. There is little that he can do for himself now. His speech is slow and somewhat garbled, but he has never lost his quick wit.

Despite his severe limitations, Vernon's ministry extends throughout the world. He is committed to the power of prayer, and through his prayers countless lives have been touched. From all across the country people call him to ask for his prayers, because they know that here is a man who will do more than talk with *them* about God. They know that Vernon will talk with *God* about them. Vernon Anderson has a significant purpose in life through the ministry of prayer.

• Yet ultimately there is only one Person who can satisfy us and restore us when we are lonely. Unless we find a meaningful relationship with God, no other step we take to cure our loneliness will be of any value. There will always be those times when we, like Jeremiah, will have no one around to support or encourage us. Only God can fully understand how we feel, and only He can really scratch our itch effectively: "The heart knows its own bitterness, and a stranger does not share its joy" (Proverbs 14:10, NASB).

The most important step we can take, when the throb of loneliness pounds relentlessly in our hearts, is this third one toward God. For only He can heal the broken heart that even time fails to mend. Because God is always near, we are never alone.

1. George Hunter, "Loneliness Is the Number One Problem in America," *National Enquirer* (March 1980).

2. Harold Ivan Smith, "Sex and Singleness the Second Time Around," *Christianity Today* (May 25, 1979).

3. Gary Collins, "Gary Collins on Loneliness," *Voices,* Trinity Evangelical Divinity School (Fall 1978):8.

4. "Living Alone," *Voices,* Fall 1978, 4-5.

Condensed by permission from *There's More to Life,* by Craig Selness. Published by Victor Books and © 1982 by SP Publications, Wheaton, Ill.

Chapter 6

The Prison of Depression

by Ruth C. Bullock

Background Scripture: Psalm 37:1-8, 39-40; Habakkuk 3:17-19

WHY DO I FEEL SO BAD all the time? I cry when I don't even know why I am crying. I can't get to sleep at night, then I am so tired I can't get up in the morning. I try to get things done, but I feel so bad, I can't even get started. I can't remember when I felt good. I'm no use to anyone. It seems so hopeless. No one seems to understand. Nothing is any fun anymore.

Have you ever had a time in your life like this? A time when you felt entombed in a prison of depression?

Sadness and crying have been part of life since man first stood up out of the dust of the earth. Sadness, when it is prolonged, and when nothing seems to make it go away, may be a sign of depression. It is conservatively estimated

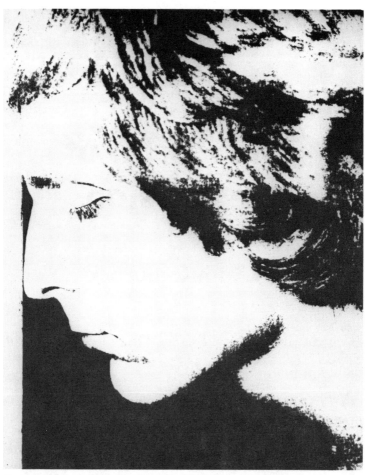

that 15 percent of the American people are depressed at any one time, and that one in three will suffer a major depression at some time in their life. We need to understand what depression is, how to recognize it, what causes it, and why it happens—even to Christians.

After King David's sin with Bathsheba and the death of their child, David felt his strength "sapped as in the heat of summer" (Psalm 32:4). He said, "My guilt has overwhelmed me like a burden too heavy to bear. . . . I am bowed down and brought very low; all day long I go about mourning. . . . I groan in anguish of heart" (38:4, 6, 8).

A biblical story of depression that most of us remember a little better is the story of Job. God said of him, "There is no one on earth like him; he is blameless and upright, a man who fears God and shuns evil" (Job 1:8). Yet Job cursed the day of his birth and said, "I have no peace, no quietness; I have no rest, but only turmoil" (3:26).

These scriptures present clear evidence of depression in the lives of both men, one depression is related to sin, and the other shows up in the life of a godly man.

If depression can visit both righteous and unrighteous, what then is the source of depression? And why is it so hard for even believers to get rid of it?

When Depression Struck the Parsonage

Marion was in her early 50s and was married to a pastor in a moderate-sized college town. The church was growing and was drawing in young couples with families. Her husband was respected both by the local church members and by other pastors in the area. Yet Marion was severely depressed. She had no energy, and she felt like crying all the time. She felt she was a burden to her family and that they would be better off without her. She had prayed, committed, and fasted. But nothing seemed to help.

Marion had married young and had raised six bright children. Her share of the ministry had been to serve as helpmate for her husband by caring for the children, cooking for the family, and doing the host of chores associated with motherhood. She was a wonderful housekeeper and had even enjoyed the assignment of cleaning the sanctuary for worship services. She had also taught Sunday School classes and led special training for the laymen courses. She loved to work.

Now the church was successful. There was a hired janitor to care for the sanctuary. There were people trained to teach Sunday School and Christian service training courses. There were others to lead the missionary society. And now that all her children were grown, the housekeeping and cooking took very little time.

Everyone told her how fortunate she was, that she could sit back and rest. What they didn't understand was that she loved serving people. She became more and more depressed; she felt sad and worthless; and she had many physical problems come up that the doctor could not explain. She did not know where to turn for hope. The cause of Marion's depression, of course, was loss, loss of a place to serve.

For Marion there was hope. She was eventually able to talk to a Christian counselor in her community. She was placed on antidepressant medication under the care of her physician. And she found a new place to use her very special skills—in an organization known as Homemakers of America. Marion began visiting the shut-ins assigned to her. She fixed their meals, cleaned their homes, did whatever they needed. And in return she found renewed health and a restored joy in the Lord. She also earned a nickname: "Sunshine Lady."

Did God answer her prayer? Sure He did. However, He did it not by cracking the skies open with lightning and instantly relieving her sadness. He did it by directing her to a Christian counseling center, which pointed her toward Homemakers of America, which assigned her to the homes of people who needed her.

We often use the term *depression* to refer to passing feelings of disappointment, which come at the end of a bad day. Such a bad mood usually lasts a few hours or a few days, then we go on with life. Blues are a part of everyone's life and are a way of dealing with the frustrations, hurts, and disappointments that are inevitable.

However, depression such as Marion experienced was more serious. It had persisted, and there was a pattern of symptoms that identify major depression. There is one other type of serious depression. It is referred to as bipolar disorder or more commonly as manic depression. You can recognize it by mood swings between depression and elation. For now, though, we are interested in major depression, the more common type of depression, which is characterized by a deep and persistent depressed mood that is free of mood swings.

Feeling of Imprisonment

Many people trapped in major depression have been there a long time, often longer than they can remember. They have tried nearly everything to pull out of it, but nothing seems to work.

They have turned to God, they have prayed, they have searched for the sin in their lives. But the sad, despairing feelings continue to thrive, while other areas of their lives begin to wither. What suffers are the jobs, the families, the friendships—all of these are neglected as the victims try to cope with the feelings of imprisonment.

Ben was what people in holiness churches call a second blessing child. He was born to a couple during their midlife years, after they had already raised two other children. So Ben was raised as an only child who became dependent on his parents. In school his father would "help" him with his projects. Actually, this meant Ben was to stay out of the way while his dad did the project "right." Even though Ben was verbally praised, actions spoke louder than words. By their actions Ben's parents were teaching him he was inadequate.

Ben was 17 when his dad died. Like Ben, the boy's mother was dependent on her husband. Now she looked to her son for strength and support. But he had not been trained to care for himself, let alone someone else. To complicate this, Ben's relatives and friends began to tell him he did not care very well for his mother. Before long, he went away to college and crashed headlong into the difficult adjustment of the first weeks. With no one to help him cope, he limped home. He later did finish school, with the help and encouragement of his wife.

Ben's wife had supported her dependent mother through a divorce and remarriage. She had been the strong one even when she was a little girl. It felt comfortable and natural to be with Ben. She did not know for years that this was because he had been trained to be helpless, and she had been trained to rescue helpless people.

Ben and his wife are working through this now, only after Ben had been depressed for years because of feelings of inadequacy. Ben felt trapped in a state of helplessness because he had been taught he needed others to do things right. Ben believed in God, and he felt called to the ministry. But he has to discover self-confidence that will displace his helpless depression. This will take a period of reeducation and a lot of support from a loving wife.

Jeff was only 18 when depression imprisoned him. He had been a star in high school, he was on the football team, active in many clubs, and president of his senior class. One of his best friends had gone to a Christian college the year before. The school had a winning football team. Now Jeff would go there too, even though the rest of the guys would be going to the local community college.

When Jeff got to college, he was only one high school star of many. And his friend had suddenly transferred to another college. Jeff did not make the varsity football team. And before long, he found that he couldn't concentrate or study. He was doing terrible in his studies. He went home as often as possible. He had not made new friends. He felt sad, lonely, and dumb. Perhaps, he thought, he just wasn't college material.

When I talked all this over with him, it became clear he was suffering from real losses and was measurably depressed. He had lost his self-esteem; he saw himself as no one special anymore—just one of many freshmen. He had lost his status. He had lost his friends. He felt like crying.

At one point he felt so sick that he actually went to the infirmary, but there was nothing physically wrong. The nurse, however, did spot the depression. Sadness, loss, sleep disturbance, diminished appetite. So we were able to help Jeff through his depression.

In many people depression shows up in physical symptoms such as headaches, stomach pains, chest pains, trouble breathing, a feeling there is something wrong—a vague feeling of being sick all over. Because physical problems can accompany depression, it is important to pay attention to the physical symptoms and to treat them.

Depression, with its physical difficulties, can overcome even people who are physically strong and in good spirits. This can happen when life tumbles in.

Sally was just such a strong person. She had been a competent young woman with a good job. She was married to a man who had a successful business making microtools from precious metals. And she had four children who were doing well in school. However, things began to change. Her husband's business began to wane, and was suddenly in danger of bankruptcy. Her mother-in-law became ill and had to move in with the family. A child the age of her daughters was murdered in the neighborhood. One of Sally's sons got into trouble with the law. And her brothers-in-law accused the family of misusing their mother's funds.

Sally got very sick. They feared she had lung cancer.

When under medical care the doctors spotted the depression and began treating both the physical symptoms and the emotional ones. Sally was placed on antidepressant medication. With the help of a counselor, she began to sort out the financial and family problems. Her husband was helped through a consumer counseling program and a small business loan. Most importantly of all, Sally found help and support in her faith and in her Christian friends.

Common Symptoms of Depression

When we think we feel the bars of major depression closing in around us, what can we do?

First, it is important to recognize the signs of depression.

A. One symptom is a down mood or a loss of interest in all or most of the favorite pastimes. An avid gardener, for example, lets the weeds take over. The mood disturbance becomes prominent and relatively persistent.

B. At least four of the following symptoms will be present nearly every day for a period of at least two weeks (in children under six, the symptoms will include at least three of the first four).

1. Poor appetite or significant weight loss (when not dieting) or increased appetite or significant weight gain. (In children under six, a signal of depression would be sounded if the child failed to make the expected weight gains that accompany normal growth.)

2. Inability to get to sleep, or early morning wakening without being able to get back to sleep. Related to this is a feeling like you can never get enough sleep, and that you need to sleep all the time.

3. Behavior slows down. The person seems to be living in slow motion or chugging along in first gear. The opposite may also be true. Behavior may be overactive, with inability to sit still.

4. Loss of interest or pleasure in usual activities. Decrease in sexual drive.

5. Loss of energy, fatigue.

6. Feelings of worthlessness, self-reproach, or excessive, inappropriate guilt.

7. Decreasing ability to concentrate. Inability to make decisions.

8. Recurrent thoughts of suicidal ideas, death, or an actual suicide attempt.

Reading such a list may be frightening to some. For others it can be reassuring that others do know what you have been feeling, what you have been afraid to tell anyone.

Perhaps you were wondering if having such feelings means you have lost your relationship with God. It is important to commit even these fears and your pain to the Lord. I find rereading Psalm 37 very helpful. Habakkuk 3:17-19 is also a favorite of many. God's promises are true, even if it doesn't feel like anyone is listening.

Second, it is important to get help.

Tell a friend, a family member, your pastor, a neighbor, or your family doctor. Then ask for help and let them get help for you. It is important for us to realize that depression makes people feel helpless and tired, and that everything seems too hard and hopeless. Therefore it will be hard for the depressed person to tell someone; it will be difficult to seek out the help that is available.

Third, recognize that there are several kinds of help available to you. Antidepressant medications are used to assist your body in fighting off depression and stress. Such medications are not addicting, though they can be misused. They are to be taken regularly as the doctor prescribes. They must be maintained at a uniform level in the body; they cannot be taken just when you feel bad.

Counseling or talking helps to sort out what went wrong. Then it is important to learn new ways of dealing with these things, should they occur again. For Marion, the pastor's wife, it meant needing new places to serve. For Ben it meant learning to take on responsibility and to trust his ability. For Jeff, who went away to college, it meant learning to cope with normal changes in life. Specifically, it meant reassessing both the need for relationships in his life as well as academic goals. For Sally, it meant legal, financial, and medical help.

If a person is in serious danger of hurting themselves, or

others, hospitalization can be a real support. There are excellent hospitals that support you until the medication and counseling can help.

More local churches, these days, are developing lists of available counselors in their area. Some counselors will be associated with Christian counseling centers, while others will be Christians who are working in local family service agencies or child guidance clinics. Denominations are beginning to do the same kind of thing, developing and maintaining a list of Christian professionals who are available throughout the country.

Family doctors also know where you can go for help. Christian television, too, is a source of good information.

If you feel trapped in a prison of depression, it is important for you to know that you are not alone and that help is available. There are keys to the prison. There is hope in Christ. God has provided healing and release directly through His grace, and through the wisdom and knowledge He has given those in the helping professions.

Ruth Bullock is chairperson of the Department of Sociology and Social Work, Azusa Pacific University, Azusa, Calif.

Chapter 7

In Search of Security

by Randall Davey

Background Scripture: Romans 8:35-39; 2 Corinthians 5:1-10

DURING SPRING BREAK recently, my wife, children, and I vanned it to the state where Bear Bryant became famous: Alabama, my wife's birthplace and now retirement home for her parents.

My in-laws had built a new home not far from Jasper, on the outskirts of a small burg called Saragosse. As soon as you cross the tracks going into town, you see the Baptist church, a cemetery, a senior center, and Edward Duncan's Store.

On the road that separates the town from the folk's place, a typical country home graces the south side of the road. A rusted pump decorates the front lawn. Shrubs and weathered trees block an otherwise clear view of the one-story house. The backdrop of woods makes the scene look more like a painting than a real-life setting.

But there is something unnatural—very unnatural: The windows and doors are covered with iron bars. Burglar bars, they're called. The lady who lives there is widowed now and wanted the bars put on the family homestead for security. So unnatural and distracting, but understandably necessary. An elderly woman living alone in the country. Insecure, and responding to it.

This lady simply went public with a fear that is common to us all. Everybody wants to be and feel secure. Much of the running-about life we live—working, spending, saving, even going to church—is done in the pursuit of security. In many respects, like ants. The South is riddled with ant-hills that are far different than the ones near my Ohio home. Instead of little piles of sand some one to two inches in height, Alabama anthills can spread out a few feet in diameter and stretch just as high. While tripping through the Saragosse cemetery, touring the Ferguson family graves, I saw more of those anthills than I could count. With the mischief of a five-year-old, I kicked a few and watched as hundreds of ants poured out of the ruined hovel, immediately responding

"Just in case, I'm wearing my swim fins."

to a life-threatening assault on their home. Driven by survival needs, they went to work repairing their security base, ignorant of my very presence.

In many respects, like ants. Driven by survival needs, we respond to life-threatening assaults.

So we retreat. Quite understandably we retreat behind iron bars of our own making. With the dead bolts locked and the chains in place, curtains drawn and the reading light on, we relax securely in a recliner and read the news. Wrong choice. For there is no escape here. On nearly every page is some word about violence and international terrorism in places you can't pronounce. Beirut: Bombings and killings. Libya: Death squads. Greece: Plane preparing to land explodes, killing three. France: Nightclub bombed, three more dead.

You shudder and thank God that you live in America, far from that kind of senseless slaughter. The Good Ol' U.S.A.: safe and secure. Then you read of three bombs going off within 17 minutes in different sections of Coeur d'Alene, Idaho. Possibly the work of white-supremacist groups. Celebrated killers—nameless thieves of life who abuse and kill innocent men, women, and children—hardly rate headline news anymore. The big news is the latest mass slaying or illogical bombing or politically based act of violence.

In sheer frustration, some of us are tempted to cancel the newspaper and restrict our viewing to reruns of the Andy Griffith show. But we can't block out the ugly reality of this violent life and untimely deaths. Fear of our own survival triggers emotional responses within the majority, who on occasion call for the execution of all robbers of life. Knowing it could be us, we scurry from place to place, buying guns and installing alarms, more locks, and burglar bars.

We can shudder only so long. We can install only so many protection devices. At some point we tend to turn our minds to more tolerable subjects. So we gather with friends for an evening of fun. And without fail, someone is the bearer of not-so-good news about the most recent tax reform, or the impending demise of Social Security, or the hopelessness of trying to save a big enough nest egg for rainy days or retirement.

All of a sudden your evening to forget it all casts you into a deeper state of despair. In all probability, you decide, terrorists will not get you, but the IRS surely will. And the *little* nest egg? You're right. It's a little nest egg, too little to give you any kind of financial security.

Well, you think, at least you have a good job. Been with the company seven years. A hard worker. That should count for something, and it does. It's a good firm. So good a major company from the East attempts a takeover. Uncertainty again. Now the future is up for grabs. You could be without a job or perhaps be moved to Salt Lake City with no say in the matter. Your paycheck is in someone's hand, and you don't even know what he looks like. Here today, what tomorrow?

And then there are insecurities related to being creatures in flawed bodies—treasures in cracked pots, some call it.

It's probably stress, you think. The chest tightens up a couple of times a day. Tough time breathing once in a while. Headaches. Nosebleeds. Understandable in light of all the uncertainty. No time to go to the doctor. Too sick to work but too broke to stay home. One more day and then it's Friday.

The last thing you remember is someone shouting, "Call 911!" Sirens. Doctors. And then deep sleep. You awaken with family members calling your name and stroking your brow. Type A personality. Bed rest for eight weeks. Can't go back to work. With your condition, it could happen again. Insecurity. Hypertension. Live or die any day doing normal, routine stuff. "Read," the doctor says. Read *what?* The *Crime Review? Terrorist Times* or the *Wall Street Journal?*

Terrorists. Neighborhood crime. Dead bolts. Economy. Health. And I haven't mentioned nukes, toxic wastes, or pollution of our ground water. And what about traumatic childhood experiences that contribute to our insecurity? Busy dads and working moms and broken homes and day-care centers that did anything but care.

We have reason to be insecure.

When you think about it, we have reason to be institutionalized. Clearly, we cannot control our present circumstances, and certainly not our future. We live under the shadow of insecurity, and we respond to the darkness in various ways.

About now, you should be asking: What to do? A talk on heaven wouldn't be a bad idea. But if the suggestions are too heavenly, we'd tend to leave them in the sky and simply continue on our stressful way. Let's try a few other suggestions.

At the heart of our insecurity is the issue of death. Some would simply say, it's the issue of our own mortality. We are going to die. Easy to say, and easy to grasp in our minds: All people die; I am a human; therefore I too shall die. The problem is I can't begin to imagine it happening to me, and neither can you. So we set about to help the winds of fate blow in some other direction. We bolt the doors, stay out of the Middle East, avoid salt and sugar, listen to relaxation tapes, and strap an air filter on our nose and a water filter on our spigot. We own our land free and clear. Raise our own vegetables and don't use artificial insecticides or growth stimulants. Work hard and save all we can, keep all we can, and invest all we can. Sorry, Brother Wesley.*

Bad news: We are going to die. Sooner or later, by hook or by crook, nuked or not, *we* are going to die. That's the worse case scenario, as finance guys say. Dead.

Another key reason for our insecurity is fear of the unknown. I was nearly at stroke level just going to kindergarten for the first time. The editor of this book, Steve

Miller, tells me that in sixth grade he prayed in all sincerity that Jesus would return before he had to begin junior high.

Death and pain and the fear of the future can paralyze us. Where can we find security in this world, anyhow?

From the Inspiring Word

Let's consult the inspired and inspiring Scripture, which serves as a guideline for living.

1. "Man is destined to die once, and after that to face judgment" (Hebrews 9:27).

This whole business of life is going somewhere. And the end is not under a shade tree by Lake Lotawana. The Bible makes it clear we will be held accountable for the ways we have responded to the Word.

2. "In this world you will have trouble. But take heart! I have overcome the world" (John 16:33).

Not just in the latter days, but throughout the ages, humanity has struggled to survive. We have to struggle because of Adam's fall, which left us all with what theologians call a bent to sinning. And that's just the beginning of trouble. Adam sinned, we've sinned, others will continue to sin. And trouble's here to stay.

3. "For I am convinced that neither death nor life, neither angels nor demons, neither the present nor the future, nor any powers, neither height nor depth, nor anything else in all creation, will be able to separate us from the love of God that is in Christ Jesus our Lord" (Romans 8:38-39).

Pretty lofty talk but true. Regardless of the source of assault, nothing can separate us from our Source of Life. So, "absent from the body, . . . present with the Lord" (2 Corinthians 5:8, KJV).

4. "So we make it our goal to please him, whether we are at home in the body or away from it" (2 Corinthians 5:9).

Our goal is not our survival; it's not living to be 103. Rather, it is to please Him who grants us pardon and life eternal so that when the time comes, whenever and however, we are ready to company with Him in the heavenlies.

5. "Be dressed ready for service and keep your lamps burning" (Luke 12:35).

Ready to go. Ready to stay. Ready to do His will. Secure in nothing or no one but Him. Secure now and evermore.

*One of Methodist founder John Wesley's famous admonitions was that we should earn all we can, save all we can, and *give* all we can.

Randall Davey is pastor of the Church of the Nazarene, Overland Park, Kans.

Chapter 8

The Fine Art of Criticizing

by Stephen M. Miller

Background Scripture: James 3:1-12

THE PREACHER thought he had a good idea for boosting Sunday School attendance.

Spring Roundup, he called it. On this one Sunday morning, everyone was supposed to dress up like cowpokes. All the kiddies—buckaroos—would get free bandannas. There would be a chuckwagon dinner after church, with all the beans and little hot doggies anyone would ever want to eat. And there would be a cowboy to do rope tricks, and even pony and wagon rides in the parking lot.

Originally, the pastor planned to have the cowboy do rope tricks on the sanctuary platform, but the church board nixed that idea and moved the trick roper to the fellowship hall. Turned loose in the sanctuary, though, were all the kids who brought to church a decorated bicycle or wagon. There was even a precharged, battery-powered Hot Wheels among the parade that zoomed up the aisles toward the altar. There, awards were presented for the most creative "floats."

The pastor got this expensive Western extravaganza past the board even though the church was several months behind in some of its bills.

I told this true vignette to my Sunday School class, then asked four of them to role-play a response to it, as though they were among the church members who had just heard the idea. Two were to criticize the pastor, and two were to defend him. The chat went something like this.

DEFENDER: I think it's a good idea.

CRITIC: But we can't afford it. And besides, it's tacky.

DEFENDER *(Pause):* But if we get a crowd, it will be worth it.

CRITIC: If you want a crowd, why not have mud wrestling?

"Hi, Baldy. I'm conducting a survey
to find out how touchy people are."

The role play turned out to be an illustration in how easy it is to criticize and how tough it is to defend. Next, I switched the players and asked the critics to become the defenders of the pastor, and the previous defenders to become the critics. The same thing happened. For the defense, it was like clawing for survival. For the prosecution, an embarrassingly easy assignment.

Through the role play, we saw how true it is that the tongue is a kind of wild animal, restless, and eager to burst out of the chute. James wrote, "No man can tame the tongue. It is a restless evil, full of deadly poison" (3:8).

Don't get me wrong. Criticism is not always bad; sometimes we have to criticize. Jesus did it, and so did Paul. So it's not *always* bad—just usually. What shoves criticism out of the white area, through the gray, and into the black is (1) our failure to recognize when to criticize and (2) our ignorance concerning how to go about it.

Before Criticizing, Ask Yourself These Questions

1. Do I have a reputation for "always having an opinion"? This is no compliment. It's a clue that you may have a knee-jerk malfunction of the mouth. Someone says or does something you don't like, and in pure reflex—without engaging your brain—you kick out your tongue.

This malfunction of the mouth seems to be a special problem for people with an aggressive temperament. In a way, the knee-jerk mouth is almost programmed into us. But with God's help, we can begin the long-term process of rewriting the program. We do this by admitting our problem and then by practicing the art of resisting the powerful temptation to throw open the chute and let the wild beast out whenever someone does something we don't like. When the chute begins to crack open, we make a conscious decision to say, "Whoa. Let's think about this. Let's get a little more information before we pass judgment." If we do this often enough, it becomes a good habit.

2. Would my comments help the person? Sometimes we criticize simply to vent our anger. This helps no one; when we blow off steam, people get burned.

One pastor I heard of got a letter from this kind of critic. The message was one word: "Fool." The pastor read it before his congregation, then said, "I've gotten a lot of anonymous letters in my day. But this is the first time I've ever gotten a letter with just the signature."

Roxanne S. Lulofs, a California teacher and housewife, faced one of these critics the day she accidentally locked her 17-month-old daughter in the car. In an article titled "The Hit-and-Run Mouth," Roxanne explains that she locked up the keys, her groceries, and the baby with one quick slam of the car door. Then she panicked and started to cry.

Firemen came and began searching for their "Slim Jim" to unlock the door, while others entertained the caged baby by making funny faces.

Then along came the hit-and-run mouth (HARM, for short). She peered through a window, swore, and exclaimed, "There's a baby in there!" She then turned to Roxanne and said, "Someone ought to kick your rear!" And she was gone.

Before we criticize, we need to evaluate our motives.

3. Would praise work better? I have a gorgeous one-year-old daughter (she looks like her mother, thankfully). And I've been puzzling over how I'm going to get the courage to discipline her when the time comes. That's why I was glad when my mom sent me an audiotape of a psychologist who explains how praise can correct behavior problems. Basically, he says we should try getting rid of the bad by praising the good.

I want you to know it works. I haven't tried it on my daughter yet, because she is still perfect. But I have tried it on my wife. I'm afraid I'm someone who likes a neat house. And my wife is someone who doesn't particularly enjoy cleaning house. Problem: I tended to criticize my wife's housekeeping and to complain that I ended up doing more than my share of it. But today I try never to gripe about this. Instead, whenever I come home from work and find the house looking as clean as you could expect of any house with a live-in, dancing whirlwind, I praise my wife with something like this: "My, this is a champion house. You've had another busy day, haven't you?"

Praise really can be an effective replacement for criticism.

4. *Have I earned the right to criticize?* If the potential target of your criticism does not respect your opinion, in most cases you might as well keep your words to yourself. Your criticism is most effective only when the person believes that you are trustworthy and that you care about them. Rule of thumb: Care first, criticize later.

5. *Do I absolutely have to criticize?* Sometimes we are too eager to do the Holy Spirit's work for Him, and we take it upon ourselves to criticize others in an effort to bring them under conviction. So we criticize and criticize and try to wear the target down with our criticism. That's called nagging. And we don't have to do it. In fact, we're not supposed to do it. The writer of Proverbs says, "Better to live out in the desert than with a nagging, complaining wife" (Proverbs 21:19, TEV). And the same goes for a nagging husband.

We can usually tell when we absolutely have to criticize. We get sick to the stomach, weak in the knees, and light in the head.

My supervisor, who was in charge of personnel, stopped by my office shortly before he and I had to talk with one of the secretaries about her poor job performance. The secretary was a timid and sensitive person, and the supervisor and I were certain she would be devastated. All day long we both dreaded the meeting. But we knew the situation had to be faced.

Besides needing to occasionally criticize the work of our subordinates, we sometimes find ourselves needing to talk frankly with our friends and spouses. The fact is, some points of difference need to be discussed, because festering wounds kill a relationship.

More common than the need to criticize in a crisis are informal invitations to criticize someone who's not around.

"What do you think of the new family in the church?"

"You've worked with Bill a long time; what's he really like?"

"Have you ever seen the pastor get mad? I mean really mad?"

These are dangerous invitations to throw open the chute and let the wild beast entertain the audience. It's dangerous because it can become backbiting. And that's sin.

Sometimes, people will really need your honest evaluation of a person or situation. But try to be objective, and present the good with the bad. In too many cases, though, your audience simply wants a little sinful entertainment at someone else's expense. So politely turn them away with something like, "I really don't know enough about that person to make a judgment."

How to Criticize

1. Be specific.

Generality: "You are a boring teacher."

Specific: "Your lessons seem heavy on the lecture and light on the discussion."

Generality: "You are unorganized."

Specific: "You misplaced three important files this week."

As a critic, deal with just one problem at a time, and focus on that single problem, not the person. The two generality statements attack the person, but the two specific statements move toward attacking the problem.

2. Assure the person that you're on his side. I can best illustrate this by telling how a friend and coworker of mine did this when he criticized me.

In a nutshell, he said, "Steve, I've heard something I think you would want me to tell you. It's about your working relationship with Sarah (not my secretary's real name). Her husband (who is a friend of my coworker) stopped me today and said he was concerned about the way you publicly humiliate his wife by correcting her in front of the other secretarial staff.

"I don't know any more than that, and I've never noticed this happening," he said, "but I thought this is something you should know."

I was shocked and not just a little embarrassed by what my colleague had said. I had long felt that my secretary was hypersensitive; so even during those times when she made serious blunders, I would climb the wall only in private and then later discuss the matter with her—after I had calmed down. And I tried to keep the discussion constructive and polite.

But as I thought about my colleague's criticism, it dawned on me that it was valid. All the secretaries work in a large room without partitions. And when we editors needed to discuss something with them, we usually just went to their desk.

I went to my secretary's desk a lot. That's because I had a lot of work. And I had to ask for a great many corrections, because my secretary was untrained and inexperienced.

Only because my friend had the courage to pass this criticism along in a kind and affirming way was I able to make the needed change in the working relationship. I simply started calling the secretary into my office whenever I needed to talk with her about her work.

3. Project an expectancy that the criticism will be accepted and dealt with successfully. In other words, think and act positively.

Try to imagine yourself in the other person's position. Accept the fact that your words may be surprising to them, so be gentle. But also realize that if you were them, you would want to hear about the problem so you could deal with it.

After you've talked, assure the person of your confidence in them. And be open to give advice, if they ask for it.

4. Rehearse what you plan to say. I find this helpful especially when there are powerful dynamics involved in the criticism: an ultrasensitive person who needs the criticism, a key issue involved, or a long-term relationship at stake—these are just a few of the knee-wobblers.

I never seem to end up saying exactly what I rehearse, sometimes not even vaguely; but this does help me to identify main points I need to discuss, and to weed out emotionally charged words and phrases. Sometimes I will even memorize an outline of what I want to say. But because criticism should quickly move from a speech to a discussion, I've never delivered my entire outline without interruption. Having it in my head, though, makes me feel a little more secure, and I do find myself returning to it during the talk.

5. Choose a good time for the criticism encounter. Even if you are the most caring of critics, don't dump your words on a person who is temporarily overdosed with the problems of life.

Finding the right time includes getting together when you are both well rested, and in a setting where you can both be as relaxed as possible.

WARNING: Even when a kindhearted, well-intentioned critic follows all these tips and the scores of others that could be added to the list, the critic could get his head handed to him on a meat platter.

It happened to my supervisor and me that day we met with the secretary I mentioned earlier. The lady was a sensitive and quiet soul who simply did not have the skills to do the work on her desk. In a series of one-on-one meetings over several months, we had discussed the specific problems in an effort to turn the situation around. But the lady was still unable to perform at the needed level of competence. The supervisor and I realized that the office needed someone else, and that the secretary needed to be freed to pursue one of many jobs for which she would be fully qualified.

We decided to place her on 30 days probation, as a last-ditch effort to turn things around. I dreaded the meeting for many reasons. To begin with, the lady seemed to have a low self-image. And I had seen her burst into tears and run from my office or the office of another editor for whom she worked, after she had been told of work she needed to redo. In addition, she had endured a tough year, with several personal traumas that would have shattered any normal person.

So I was expecting in this meeting to see her disintegrate before my eyes, even though the supervisor and I would be as kind as honesty would allow.

Well, I was wrong.

She peeled off the angel fish scales and revealed a barracuda. She went home that night and wrote a four-page, single-spaced letter in which she filleted me, my supervisor, and the entire charitable organization for which she worked. Then she threatened to sue us for harassment. She sent copies of this letter to everyone she thought would be interested, including our chief executive officer.

Eventually she resigned the position. But the weeks that followed her letter of retaliation were tense for everyone involved.

Criticism is a risky business. In fact, it can be a killer. Remember Patrick Henry Sherrill, the 44-year-old postal worker in Edmond, Okla.? On Tuesday, August 19, 1986, a supervisor criticized Sherrill's work and threatened to fire him. On Wednesday morning, Sherrill walked into the post office and methodically killed 14 coworkers, wounded 8 others, then killed himself.

We can never know exactly how someone will respond

to our critical words. Most people will not lose control and physically injure themselves or others. But we can count on the fact that they will be surprised, embarrassed, and hurt. Sometimes, though, this short-term heartache is worth the long-term joy that comes after working through the problem.

Truth: Criticizing is like open-heart surgery. If you have to do it, be careful. If you don't have to do it, don't. If there's someone better able and willing to do the hacking, don't pick up the scalpel.

Stephen M. Miller is electives editor for the Church of the Nazarene Headquarters in Kansas City.

Chapter 9

The Price Tag for Envy

by Lloyd John Ogilvie

Background Scripture: 1 Samuel 18:1-9; James 4:1-10

AN ANCIENT GREEK LEGEND tells of an athlete who ran well but placed only second. The crowd applauded the winner, and eventually a statue was erected in his honor. Meanwhile, the one who had placed second came to think of himself as a loser. Envy ate away at him, filling his body with stress. He could think of nothing else but his defeat and his lust to be number one. So he decided to destroy the statue that daily reminded him of his lost glory.

Cautiously he began to implement his plan. Late each night, he went to the statue and chiseled at the base to weaken the foundation. One night, however, as he chiseled in violent and envious anger, he went too far. The heavy marble statue teetered on its fragile base and crashed down on the disgruntled athlete. He died beneath the crushing weight of the marble replica of the one he had grown to hate.

But in reality, he had been dying long before, inch by inch, chisel blow by chisel blow. He was the victim of his own competitive envy.

One of the major causes of stress today is combative competition—more accurately, envy. Rooted in a lack of self-esteem, it grows in the soul-soil of comparisons and blossoms in noxious thorns of desire for what others have.

Envy and jealousy are sleepless bedfellows who keep each other awake day and night in their fitful agitation. Their restlessness, in turn, keeps us agitated, under stress.

An executive recently told me about one of his employees: "If that guy ever stopped working so hard at pretending he's working, he'd get ahead. Problem is, he's always taking his own success pulse, comparing himself and his job with others. He's not a keen competitor, he's a combative one. He works so hard at looking great, he'll never be great. Truth is, he doesn't need to pretend to compete. He's got what it takes. All he needs to do is affirm his own potential, stop worrying about what others do, and get moving."

I asked my friend if he'd ever said that to the younger man. He laughed. "No, I haven't," he said. "I know I should.

But then, he'd probably get moving so fast he'd be in place for my job!"

Both men were suffering from envy. But the one who could so incisively analyze the other was not aware of his own attitude.

Competition isn't bad if it prompts us to pull out all the stops and live at our own full potential. But stress surges within us when we want to beat others rather than do our best. It eats away at us when we begin to take our readings from other people.

L. B. Flynn, in *You Can Live Above Envy*, puts it plainly: "The envious man feels others' fortunes are his misfortunes; their profit, his loss; their blessing, his bane; their health, his illness; their promotion, his demotion; their success, his failure."

This attitude leads to negative criticism. There boils within us something of the spirit of the rhyme: "I hate the guys who minimize and criticize the other guys whose enterprise has made them rise above the guys who criticize." We've all been both the critical and the criticized. Both cause excruciating stress, and we must ask ourselves: What can we do about what that does to us and others?

The answer is found in an excellent stress management manual—the Book of James. James saw envy and competition as a tragic threat to the early Christians. He asked and answered a crucial question: "What causes fights and quarrels among you? Don't they come from your desires that battle within you?" (4:1).

The word *desires,* used in this verse, does not mean just sensual or material lust. It also refers to the drive for recognition and success. James launches a full-scale attack against the insecurity within us that forces us to take our value signals from a comparison of others.

At times we've all experienced insecurity that overwhelms us because someone else is outdoing us. We are spurred on not so much to reach the goals God has given us as to outdistance others. It becomes a no-win marathon against others—really against ourselves. Others must be pushed down or tripped up in their race of life for us to be out ahead.

Healthy competition in a sport or business, however, can be a part of the fun of life—with wins and losses. Every great athlete and successful business person wins when the goal is to do his very best. In those high moments the purpose is not to defeat the competition, but to produce at maximum. It may result in a better score or product or service than our colleagues achieve, but in no way does it minimize their accomplishments.

The focus of James's concern is what envious competition does to our relationships. It denies Christ's victory over sin and death by substituting our values for His. We keep running a race we've already won through Calvary. We take our readings from others rather than Christ and His victory for all of us. Hence, we become silent antagonists of one another rather than enthusiastic members of one another's cheering section.

Thoughtless, insensitive comparisons pit us against others; we put them down in an effort to bolster ourselves. When this happens in the church, it becomes a house of judgment instead of fellowship and mutual esteem and encouragement. Strife and stress replace peace and unity.

Billy Graham was right when he said, "Envy can ruin reputations, split churches, and cause murders. Envy can shrink our circle of friends, ruin our business, and dwarf our souls . . . I have seen hundreds cursed by it."

The stress of envious competition has been around for a long time. Cain murdered Abel because of it. Joseph's brothers tried to murder him because of the virulent poison of their competition. Envy set Aaron against his brother Moses. Saul was a burning caldron of envious instability because of David's victories. The disciples competed with one another for first place in Jesus' attention.

Christian history displays a despicable record of denominational strife. And even the most pious of Christians have consistently envied each other's spiritual growth or accomplishments. Envious competition is Satan's power tool to separate those who should be inseparable participants in the grace of Christ.

But James penetrates into the deeper cause of envy. He calls it lust for what we do not have. We covet the opportunities and skills of others, which seem to exceed our own. We then miss becoming the unique, special persons the Lord has created each of us to be.

The secret of managing that stress is to ask for the Lord's help. James says, "You do not have, because you do not ask God" (4:2).

We are to ask for the Lord's goals for us and the power to accomplish them. The Lord does not play favorites or pit us against one another. He is for us, not against us. We can ask Him: "Lord, who am I? What do You want me to do? What are Your resources to accomplish Your vision for my life?" This is the antidote to envy.

Recently I talked to a man who was critical of a "friend." He cut him to pieces with harsh judgment. I sensed something more than righteous indignation.

"Have you ever wished you were in this person's shoes?" I asked. "Ever wished you had his opportunities and challenges?" A flow of jealousy then drained from a cesspool of envy.

The two men had been rivals for years. The other man always seemed to be out ahead. Life had been so much easier for him, my friend said. He never realized he was envious.

But it would have done no good to tell him to stop being envious. The causes were deep-rooted in his own lack of self-affirmation.

Mustering up courage and drawing from my own experience, I said, "Until you let God love you profoundly—to the point of excitement over your uniqueness—you will shift this envy from one person to another. There always will be someone who seems to have more than you."

I had touched a raw nerve. Blood rushed to his face. I dared to cause stress in that moment to help him find a cure for a greater stress than envy: "You will be envious of others until you get converted!"

The man was a church member, and at that moment he got very angry. "What do you mean?" he said with a tone of a wounded animal.

"The result of being loved by God is self-acceptance," I said. "Feeling good about ourselves is the sure sign that we have been converted from self-hate to constructive self-appreciation. You are special, and so is your friend. Love for him, with all his hang-ups, will flow out of the well of a new self-image. Ask God what He wants you to be and do. You are not racing against your friend, but for God's goal."

The prompting of God's Spirit in that moment resulted in his openness to what had been said. We prayed together, asking for the Lord's plan and the power to fix his sight on God's destination, not on other people.

James goes on to cite envy as the cause of our committing adultery with the world—a potent image. James warns that that's the outcome when our desire for something or someone vies with our love for God.

The solution to destructive jealousy may startle us. It's to experience the creative jealousy of God. Scripture is filled with the Lord's own words to declare His unwillingness to accept any role except that of the Lord. The very nature of His Lordship demands that it cannot be shared with any other. "I, the Lord your God, am a jealous God" (Exodus 20:5).

Having been married to God by His call and commission, we belong first and only to Him. When we desire worldly goals more than Him, we enter into a competing love relationship. When we put success, recognition, and personal desires above Him, we become adulterous. We idolize the world's standards and thus are drawn into envious competition.

When we envy others, we fail to understand how much Christ loves and cherishes us. We don't have to be like any other person, do what he does, or love what rightfully belongs to someone else. Combative competition is the result of our uneasy state of grace. We judge others to exalt ourselves. But our putdowns put down only one party—ourselves.

James advises: "Humble yourselves before the Lord, and he will lift you up" (4:10). When we accept ourselves as the special individuals God made us to be, we can rest in the fact that the Lord will multiply our potential beyond our wildest imagination. An honest recognition of our assets and liabilities multiplied by His indwelling power equals excellence without stress.

From *Making Stress Work for You,* by Lloyd J. Ogilvie, copyright ©
1984, as it appeared in *Moody Monthly;* used by permission of Word Books, Publisher, Waco, Tex.

Chapter 10

Owning Anger: Let Both Your Faces Show

by David Augsburger

Background Scripture: Mark 3:1-6

YOUR WIFE made a cutting remark two days ago, and still no apology. Your daughter didn't thank you for the little gift you bought her. Your son forgot to put the tools back in their place in your shop. And you're feeling angry at all of them, at everything!

Anger is a demand.

Like, "I demand an apology from you—an apology that suits me."

"I demand you show appreciation for my gifts—in a way that pleases me."

"I demand that you return my tools—perfectly—just the way I keep them."

Even though you seldom put the demands into words, they are there inside your feelings. And you are resentful.

Freedom from being dominated by anger begins by tracking down the demands made on others. Recognizing them, admitting them out loud speeds up the process of owning the anger. Then one has a choice: (1) to negotiate the demands that matter, or (2) to cancel the ones that don't.

Freedom comes as one is candid and open in facing the demands made on others. Wisdom comes as one is willing to cancel unfair demands. Maturity comes through freeing others to live and grow without the imposition of controlling demands.

Recognized or unrecognized, the demands are there. Anger is a demand. It may be a demand that you hear me. Or that you recognize my worth. Or that you see me as precious and worthy to be loved. Or that you respect me. Or let go of my arm. Or quit trying to take control of my life.

"Do you want to talk about it?"

The demands emerge whenever I see you as rejecting me, or foresee you as about to reject me as a person of worth.

Actually, I first feel anxious. "Anxiety is a sign that one's self-esteem, one's self-regard is endangered," as Harry Stack Sullivan expressed it.[1] When my freedom to be me is threatened, I become anxious, tense, ready for some action. Escape? Anger? Or work out an agreement?

Escape may be neither possible nor practical. Agreement seems far away since I see you as ignoring my freedom, devaluing my worth, and attempting to use me. Anger is the most available option.

Anger is "the curse of interpersonal relations," Sullivan well said. A curse, because it is so instantly effective as a way of relieving anxiety. When a person flashes to anger, the anger clouds his recall of what just happened to spark the anger, confuses his awareness of what he is really demanding, and restricts his ability to work toward a new agreement.

But we chose—consciously or unconsciously—to become angry because:

"Anger is much more pleasant to experience than anxiety. The brute facts are that it is much more comfortable to feel angry than anxious. Admitting that neither is too delightful, there is everything in favor of anger. Anger often leaves one sort of worn out . . . and very often makes things worse in the long run, but there is a curious feeling of power when one is angry."[2]

Check the pattern: (1) I feel keen frustration in my relationship with another. (2) I see the other person as rejecting me—my worth, my needs, my freedom, my request. (3) I become suddenly and intensely anxious. (4) I blow away my anxiety with anger which confuses things even further. (5) I may then feel guilty for my behavior and resentful of the other's part in the painful experience.

Anxiety is the primary emotion. It signals that a threat is received, a danger is perceived, or a devaluation has been "subceived" (subconsciously received) in another's response to me.

Anger is a secondary emotion. It signals that demands are being expressed toward the source of pain, hurt, frustration.

If I own my anxiety and deal constructively with my demands, my anxious arousal and my angry appraisal of the situation can be used to renegotiate relationships until they are mutually satisfactory.

You're standing in the living room, looking out the window at your son's back. You're replaying the last moment's conversation. "How stupid can you get?" you'd said. "You blew it again like a no-good kid. That's what you are, and you better shape up or you're shipping out."

There he goes, anger and rejection showing in the slump of his shoulders. "He blew it?" you asked yourself. "Well, I blew it even worse. I get angry, I attack him personally, I put him down, I chop away at his self-esteem. I'm getting nowhere. What else can we do? If I could just deal with what he's doing without attacking him. Maybe that would make a difference. I could try it."

When I am on the receiving end of another's anger, I want to hear the anger-messages the other gives to me, and check out what I am picking up as a demand. Careful listening can discern what the other is demanding, clarify it in clear statements, and lead to clean confrontation. Then I have the choice of saying yes to the other's demands, or saying no. I may feel angry in return, but I want to experience my anger with honest "I statements," not with explosive "you statements."

Explosive anger is powerless to effect change in relationships. It dissipates needed energies, stimulates increased negative feelings, irritates the other persons in the transaction, and offers nothing but momentary discharge. Vented anger may ventilate feelings and provide instant, though temporary, release for tortured emotions, but it does little for relationships.

Clearly expressed anger is something different. Clear statements of anger feelings and angry demands can slice through emotional barriers or communications tangles and establish contact.

When angry, I want to give clear, simple "I messages." "You messages" are most often attacks, criticisms, devaluations of the other person, labels, or ways of fixing blame.

"I messages" are honest, clear, confessional. "I messages" own my anger, my responsibility, my demands without placing blame. Note the contrast between honest confession and distorted rejection.

I Messages	You Messages
I am angry.	You make me angry.
I feel rejected.	You're judging and rejecting me.
I don't like the wall between us.	You're building a wall between us.
I don't like blaming or being blamed.	You're blaming everything on me.
I want the freedom to say yes or no.	You're trying to run my life.
I want respectful friendship with you again.	You've got to respect me or you're not my friend.

Anger energies become a creative force when they are employed (1) to change my own behavior which ignored the other's preciousness and (2) to confront the other with his need to change unloving behavior. Anger energy can be directed at the cause of the anger, to get at the demands I am making, to own them, and then either correct my demanding self by canceling the demand, or call on the other to hear my demand and respond to how I see our relationship and what I want.

Focusing anger on the person's behavior frees one to stand with the other even as you stand up for your demands.

The freedom to express appreciation for the other as a person, even as you explain your anger at his way of behaving, lets you stay in touch while getting at what you are angry about. You can be both angry (at behaviors) and loving (toward persons) at the same time.

Anger erupted in a place of worship, the synagogue.

A handicapped man with paralysis of the hand came asking Jesus for healing. The religious leaders are (1) looking on with malice, (2) anticipating that Jesus may break their ceremonial blue laws against doing a service for another on the Sabbath, (3) hoping for some such infraction of the law so they can charge Him with illegal, irreligious, irresponsible action.

Jesus avoids neither the man in need nor His own critics.

"Stand up and come out here in front," He says to the man.

Then He turns to the Pharisees. He is aware of their demands—demands characteristic of many religious leaders through the centuries—(1) that principles come before the pain of persons, (2) that religious piety be honored above the needs of a brother, (3) that legalistic obedience is more important than human life and love for others. Jesus focuses their demands in the kind of question-statements they were so fond of debating. "What is truly right, just, good? To do good or to do evil on the Sabbath? To save life or to destroy it?" But in acting so, He is clearly confronting and refusing their demands.

There is silence. (As an answer, silence is often violence.)

Jesus is deeply hurt at their inhumanity.

He looks at them in anger. His look sweeps from one face to another. His demand is clear. Be human. Be loving. Care about people. Respect this man's needs. See him as precious.

Then Jesus does the responsible, loving, caring thing. "Stretch out your hand," He says to the man.

He stretches it out, and it is as sound as the other (Mark 3:1-6, paraphrased from Phillips).

That is clear, focused, creative, controlled, dynamic anger.

Hate is sin	Love is virtue
Anger is evil	Affection is good
Confronting is brutal	Caring is wonderful
Openness is questionable	Diplomacy is wise

Do you find yourself thinking in such clearly defined categories? Rejecting hate, anger, honest awareness, and expression of your true feelings and perspectives and clear confrontation with others? To cut off one-half of your emotional spectrum and reject all negative feelings is to refuse to be a whole person. To deny and repress everything on the negative side is to also stifle and crush the full expression of your positive side.

There is danger in abusing and misusing others with our positive emotions and actions—love, kindness, gentleness, tolerance, sweetness—just as there is the threat of cutting and destroying others with our negative responses—anger, harshness, criticism, irritation. To be engulfed and incorporated by a smothering love, all sweet gentleness, and I'm-only-trying-to-help-you-it's-for-your-own-good kindness is more treacherous than harsh, crisp frankness. You can at least reject frankness without fighting an affectionate, sticky mass of divinity-candy love.

To be a whole person in relationships, risk sharing both sides of yourself. Be open with both your negatives (honest anger) and your positives (affirming love). Let both your faces show. There are two sides in everyone. Both sides are important. Both are acceptable. Both are precious. Both can be loved.

We prefer to think that God wants our very best and only our best; that God will have nothing to do with weakness, timidity, or fears.

Not so. God accepts weakness as well as strength, fear as well as confidence, anger as well as gentleness.

God loves whole persons.

Such love makes wholeness possible in its most complete form. As we know and experience the love of God, His acceptance reaches out to include both sides of us. "God knows the best and worst about us; and what do you know? God loves us anyway."

I can be aware of my feelings of anger. (I am accepted.)

I can own my resentments, my hate, my hostility. (I am loved.)

I can discover new ways of experiencing my negative and my positive feelings. (I am free to grow.)

I can be angry in creative, loving, caring ways. (I see it modeled in Jesus.)

Harry's been your friend for years. You could always count on him. Now you hurt him. He's turned against you. Last month it was Steve. You cut him off in an angry moment; it hasn't been the same. People you've been close to for years now hold you at a distance.

"So what. If they want to let me down, who needs them," you tell yourself. But inside you say, "I need them. I want their friendship. But I drive them away from me. It's like I've been carrying an overload of anger in my gut.

"I've got to talk it out with someone," you tell yourself. But where do you turn? "I need to talk to someone about who to talk to," you say. "Maybe my minister would listen to me and suggest where I could find out what's bothering me."

(When you find yourself carrying an overload of anger as extra baggage, talk it out with someone you trust—a friend, your minister, your doctor. And reach out to others for new ways of respectful behaving that get you where you really want to be with your friends.)

"I just can't help it. It makes me angry."

"It just gets to me and touches off my temper."

"It's like something comes over me, and I can't do a thing about it."

"It's other people, that's what it is. They know I've got a quick temper and they're out to get me."

"It" is the problem. "It" causes untold irritation, anger, frustration, embarrassment, pain, guilt, and misery. "It" is not me. "It" is this something, or someone, or some situation.

When you find yourself using "it" as an explanation or as a scapegoat, stop. Listen to yourself. Recognize what you're doing: avoiding responsibility; sidestepping the real problem; denying ownership of your feelings, responses, and actions.

Release comes not from denying but from owning who—what—and where I am in my relationships.

I want to own what goes on in me and accept total responsibility for it.

I discover that as I own it, accepting full responsibility, I am then able to respond in new ways. I become response-able.

A great freedom comes as I own my thoughts, feelings, words, and emotions: (1) I become free to choose my actions; (2) I become free to choose my reactions.

My actions are mine. Your actions are yours. I am responsible for my behavior. You are responsible for yours.

I also accept responsibility for my actions.

"You make me angry," I used to say.

Untrue. No one can make another angry. If I become angry at you, I am responsible for that reaction. (I am not saying that anger is wrong. It may well be the most appropriate and loving response that I am aware of at that moment.)

But *you* do not make me angry. *I* make me angry at you. It is not the only behavior open to me.

There is no situation in which anger is the only possible response. If I become angry (and I may, it's acceptable) it's because I choose to respond with anger. I might have chosen kindness, irritation, humor, or many other alternatives (if I had been aware of these choices). There is no situation which commands us absolutely. For example, I have the choice to respond to another's threat with blind obedience, with silent passivity, with vocal refusal, with firm resistance, or with anger, if that seems appropriate.

When childhood experiences are limited, a person may mature with a limited set of behaviors open to him. Some have only two ways of coping with another's attack—anger or submission. If these are the only ways modeled by the parents or the family, they may be the only aware-choices in the person's behavioral repertoire.

If I have grown enough in life so that more than one pattern of behavior is available to me, then I can freely select the responses which seem most appropriate to the situation.

I want to be aware of a wealth of responses and to have them available to me. Anger or patience. Toughness or gentleness. Clear confrontation or warm, caring support. I want to be able-to-respond in any of these.

I am responsible for choosing my responses to you.

I am responsible for the way I react to you.

I am responsible for how I see you. And from the way I see you—as either friendly or hostile, accepting or rejecting, welcoming or threatening—emerge my feelings. Feelings are the energies that power the way I choose to see you or to perceive you.

I am responsible for how I see you—and from that for the way I feel about you.

You cannot make me angry. Unless I choose to be angry.

You cannot make me discouraged or disgusted or depressed. These are choices.

You cannot make me hate. I must choose to hate.

You cannot make me jealous. I must choose envy.

I experience all these and more on all too many occasions, but I am responsible for those actions or reactions. I make the choice.

And I am free to choose loving responses. I am free to choose trusting replies. I am free to react in concerned, understanding ways if I choose to see the other person as precious, as valuable, as worthy of love because he is equally loved of God.

I love me.

I love my freedom
    to be who I am.

I love my drive
    to be all I can be.

I love my right
    to be different from you.

I love my need
    to be related to you.

I also love you.

I respect your freedom
    to be who you are.

I admire your drive
    to be all you can be.

I recognize your right
    to be different from me.

I appreciate your need
    to be related to me.

The thoughts I think,
The words I speak,
The actions I take,
The emotions I feel—
    They are mine. For them
    I am fully responsible.

The thoughts you think,
The words you speak,
The actions you take,
The emotions you feel—
    They are yours. For
    them I am in no way
    responsible.

I am free
to accept or to refuse
    your wants
    your requests
    your expectations
    your demands.

I can say yes.

I can say no.

I am not in this world
    to live as you prescribe.

You are free
to accept or to refuse
    my wants
    my requests
    my expectations
    my demands.

You can say yes.

You can say no.

You are not in this world
    to live as I prescribe.

I am not responsible
    for you.

You are not responsible
    for me.

I will not be
    responsible *to* you.
	You need not be
	    responsible *to* me.

I want to be
    responsible *with* you.
	You can be
	    responsible *with* me.

1. Harry Stack Sullivan, *The Psychiatric Interview* (New York: W. W. Norton, 1954), 218-19.

2. Ibid., 109.

Chapter 11

Getting Along with Others

by Jon Johnston

Background Scripture: Hebrews 12:14; 1 John 3:11-24

WE'VE SEEN the little, rotund creatures lumber away from us at the zoo. Their body is a pincushion of sharp quills. Few of us would even consider adopting one as a pet. It's pretty tough to express affection to a moving cactus.

But before giving porcupines any more bad press, we must admit that some humans are just as uninviting. To get close to them is to invite mental anguish. They needle us with insults, puncture us with complaints, stick us with criticisms, and jab us with accusations.

Have any names or faces popped into your mind? One looms in my own consciousness right now. She deserves to be inducted into the "Human Porcupine Hall of Fame." Let me tell you about a memorable encounter I had with her.

My wife, Cherry, and I began serving a church as members of the staff. Before long we discovered that a young

"*Now, Mrs. Hooper, tell the court what happened when you and your neighbor argued over the electric hedge clippers.*"

couple on the staff was having a great deal of trouble relating with persons in the church, including the other staff. They were openly critical and unashamedly defiant. In fact, they took it upon themselves to tell new converts to immediately shape up their lives—or else. They created such an uproar that, according to the grapevine, they were about to be fired.

Cherry and I moved onto the scene, determined to help this couple. We were optimistic that things could turn around. So we invited the couple for dinner, and we sensed they were truly enjoying themselves. But about the time we had almost finished our meal, the young wife looked across the table at Cherry and said: "You're one person I can't stand at all. And it's because you always look so happy." The woman was deadly serious. And her hostility was clearly displayed in both the sharp tone of her voice and the squint of her eyes.

The quill was deeply implanted. My wife and I were demolished.

It became painfully clear to us why this abrasive woman was having such difficulty cultivating meaningful relationships. And we weren't to be her last victims. One by one, others were assaulted. Many of them stopped coming to our church before this woman and her husband finally left.

This is just one story about one human porcupine. How widespread is the proliferation of human porcupines?

May Their Tribe Decrease

In our "me first" era, there is no shortage of discourteous and aggressive people. And their numbers seem to be increasing.

Just try changing lanes on a freeway. Drivers behind you, who assume they own the lane you wish to enter, are likely to speed up.

At a ball game, gently ask the person in front of you to sit down so that you can see. A fellow who sat next to me at a Dodger game did this very thing. Result: The man who received the gentlemanly request immediately pulled out his switchblade and said: "One more comment out of you, and I'll put your lights out!" No more comments from the gentleman. And the man with a fondness for switchblades just kept standing.

How about church? If there is any place on earth where people should get along with people, it is in God's house and with God's people. And that's what always happens. Right? Not hardly.

The church environment is ripe for conflict. Why? Factors include overfamiliarity, overwork (with accompanying stress), taking one another for granted, and devious power plays. At times things can become quite savage.

Should abrasiveness be excused among God's people?

Should we pass it off with comments like: "People will be people"; "God gives some of us an uneven temperament"; or "We all have our off days"?

The answer is no, according to God's Word. We are told to let the peace of God rule our hearts (Colossians 3:15), to be at peace among ourselves (1 Thessalonians 5:13), and to follow peace with all men (Hebrews 12:14). War is to be waged against Satan and sin, but not against those for whom Jesus died.

We really need to get along with our Christian brothers and sisters. Intramural squabbles affect the church more than we can realize. When people stop attending, usually fictitious reasons are given: the need for a better youth program for their teens, "I feel led," "I just need a change." But usually people leave for one major reason: They are not getting along with others. They have been wronged, and as a result, love webs have been broken. (Or in some cases they were never really formed.)

John puts it plainly: "But whoever hates his brother is in the darkness" (1 John 2:11). Then, we are told: "And this is his command: to believe in the name of his Son, Jesus Christ, and to love one another" (3:23).

Jesus once declared: "By this all men will know that you are my disciples, if you love one another" (John 13:35).

But how is this love exemplified in our daily walk? What specific suggestions will help us continually improve and refine our relationships with others?

Dale Carnegie once wrote a best-selling book titled *How to Win Friends and Influence People.* Our question to ourselves, as Christians, is similar. In what ways can we "influence friends and win people" (to Jesus Christ)?

Metamorphosis: From Porcupine to Dove

A fiesty blue jay lives in one of our trees. He attacks all moving objects that approach "his territory," from tomcats to mailmen. He swoops down with claws extended, making a terrible racket, and he often ends up losing more than a few of his tail feathers.

God's Word tells us to be as "harmless as doves" (Matthew 10:16, KJV). Never have I observed an attacking dove. Rather, the dove is peaceful, gentle, nonaggressive. And it presents us with a beautiful illustration for our own lives.

Being dovelike means avoiding certain things. As Christians, since our goal is to be truly peaceful, we will reject being any of the following:

1. OBLIVIOUS: retreating into "our world," to the exclusion of others

2. OBNOXIOUS: becoming offensive, thereby alienating others

3. OSTENTATIOUS: seeking to impress, in a manner that puts people down, in order to elevate ourselves

But to know what to avoid is not enough. We must become aware of, and constantly strive toward, positive standards. Standards that characterized the life of our Lord. Standards that His Word instructs us, as His followers, to embrace. Standards that will help us become the salt and the light in a decaying, darkened world.

Let's focus on some of these worthwhile standards.

Rx for Becoming People People

First, we must dare to reach out to others, even though we're likely to experience some failure and rejection. We must not wait for others to embrace us; rather, we must assertively and lovingly move toward them. According to psychologist Phillip Zimbardo, shyness is a disease that insures defeat and eventual depression. It must be vigorously countered in our lives, even if it feels unnatural to do so.

Jesus continually reached out to others, even though many rejected His overtures. Listen to His words: "O Jerusalem . . . how often I have longed to gather your children together, as a hen gathers her chicks under her wings, but you were not willing" (Matthew 23:37).

In spite of this rejection, our Master continued to reach out to the lowly, the downcast, the losers, the ones who could do nothing for Him. And He still does. In doing so, He provides us with our Example.

Second, in reaching out, we must do much more listening than talking. As someone declared, God gave us two ears and only one mouth for a reason—to show us that we should do twice as much listening as we do talking.

I cannot help but think of the Gadarene, who lived among the tombstones. When this demon-possessed man spoke to Jesus, the Lord listened intently. It may have been the first time anyone had paid the Gadarene this kind of respect. Jesus listened to him. He listens to us too. Likewise, we must do the same.

Listening requires us to focus our attention on the other person rather than on ourselves. And Philippians tells us that doing so is an important component of the Christian style (2:3-4). We are told to esteem others better than ourselves and possess lowliness of mind. Furthermore, rather than focusing on our own interests, our primary attention must be on others.

We pay others a great courtesy when we care enough to truly listen—to listen to their innermost feelings, as well as to their words. Not incidentally, such persons become more open to our Christian message after we have heard them voice their own ideas and sentences.

Third, we must be accepting rather than judgmental. Often our minds race toward conclusion drawing, categorizing, judging.

Remember the words of Jesus, when the accusers brought the woman who was caught in the act of adultery? Turning to the accusers, He declared: "If any one of you is without sin, let him be the first to throw a stone at her"

(John 8:7). They slowly disappeared, until only the accused remained. Jesus looked at her and, after agreeing that they no longer condemned her, declared, "Neither do I . . . Go now and leave your life of sin" (v. 11).

How often we demand accountability before we offer acceptance, and that only causes people to stumble.

Joaquin Miller's poem "In Men Who Condemn" contains a great truth:

> In men, whom men condemn as ill,
> I find so much of goodness still.
> In men whom men pronounce divine,
> I find so much of sin and blot,
> I dare not draw a line between the two,
>   where God has not.

Fourth, we must master the art of tact. Being brutally frank is OK only if we wish to be a brute. We must be acutely sensitive to others' feelings. Again, our mission is to be as gentle as a dove.

The diplomacy and tact of Jesus was astounding. He never invaded the privacy of anyone. Never did He coerce. He entreated rather than shamed. Why? Because He wanted people to choose Him freely and with personal conviction.

So many tactless acts occur within the church. Our comments often throw people on the defensive. ("Where have you been for the last three Sundays?" "Your interpretation of the Bible is completely wrong!" "But you didn't graduate from a Christian college, therefore you're at a real disadvantage in understanding this particular lesson." "When are you going to stop letting your kid control you?")

If only we could hear ourselves or feel the painful impact that we make on the lives of others.

Fifth, we must produce generous doses of humor. Humor is the oil that lubricates human relationships. When we laugh together, our ties become cemented—provided that the target of our laughter is appropriate.

Elton Trueblood has written a fine book on the humor of Jesus. Our Lord manifested this quality in numerous instances. For example, Jesus spoke of the Pharisees trying to pluck the splinter from the eye of others before pulling the plank from their own eyes. He exemplified humor by exaggeration—one of the funniest kinds.

Although we must take our work and mission seriously, we are well admonished to not take ourselves too seriously. Laughter directed toward ourselves can cultivate humility. Also, it can encourage others to be less defensive and more transparent. In short, more real.

Finally, although our relationships may be precious to us, we must always be willing to let go. When we cling to people as the source of our security, when we smother them with our overprotection, when we continue to grieve after their departure, we set in motion the weather pattern for a spiritual drought.

The prayer of relinquishment is, indeed, necessary for our lives. In His high priestly prayer, Jesus relinquished His control over His disciples (John 17). He placed them in the hands of His Heavenly Father, unbegrudgingly and lovingly.

Letting go should not be a morbid occasion. Listen to these wise words by writer Barbara Johnson:

> To let go is not to cut myself off, it's to realize that I cannot control another.
> To let go is to admit powerlessness, which means the outcome is not in my hands.
> To let go is not to judge, but to allow another to be.
> To let go is not to deny but to accept.
> To let go is not to regret the past, but to grow and live for the future.
> To let go is to fear less and to love more.

The ability to get along with others is valuable indeed. Of course, sometimes conflict seems unavoidable. There are what one person I know calls "irregular people." These are folks who make a concerted effort to give us misery. Just like the 40 irregular people who vowed to kill the apostle Paul, and the one irregular disciple who betrayed our Lord.

From such experiences, however, we can learn important lessons, not the least of which is patience. Suffering is inevitable, especially when it comes to our relationships. We need only recall that Jesus learned obedience through the things He suffered (Hebrews 5:8). Likewise, we must learn obedience, for it is an integral component of our love for God. And if that requires painful relationships, so be it.

Nevertheless, it is imperative that we admonish ourselves with these words: "Live in peace with all men" (Hebrews 12:14). To the very best of our ability, and with His power, we must seek to cultivate healthy, fulfilling, Christ-centered relationships with everyone.

Does anyone fit this pattern? Is there a person who embodies the principles that we have advocated? Yes, and she attends our church.

Norma Is Her Name

Norma has had more than her share of setbacks. An aged father lives close by and depends on her for care. Her children have experienced great difficulty in their marriages. She has always been there to help and encourage. She has had to pitch in to rejuvenate her husband's plumbing business. And just recently, she underwent a painful operation to remove a malignant growth from the side of her face.

Nevertheless, Norma is not one to complain. The sunshine of her smile and warm personality just continue to radiate, bringing warmth to all she encounters. Her words are kind and uplifting. She is extremely generous. (One of her favorite acts is to buy Dodger tickets and give them away.) And her laughter is the heartiest of anyone I know.

Norma enjoys life, and she does all she can to help others do the same. Best of all, the peace of Jesus fills her heart.

We, too, have the potential for becoming a Norma, but in our own way. We can possess such a warmth of spirit that people will be drawn to us and to the Savior we love. Let's give God an opportunity to cultivate this necessary quality in our lives.

Even on his best day, a porcupine doesn't have a chance against a dove.

Jon Johnston is professor of sociology at Pepperdine University, Malibu, Calif.

Chapter 12

Loving the Ugly

by Al Truesdale

Background Scripture: Matthew 25:31-46; 2 Corinthians 5:16-20

THE PHONE RANG in a wealthy Boston home. On the other end of the line was a son calling from California. He had just returned from Vietnam. The young man said to his mother, "I just called to tell you that I want to bring a buddy home with me."

His mother said, "Sure, bring him along for a few days."

"But Mother, there is something you need to know about this boy. One leg is gone, one arm is missing, one eye's gone, and his face is disfigured. Is it all right if I bring him home?"

His mother answered, "Bring him home for just a few days."

The son continued, "You don't understand, Mother. I want to bring him home to live with us." As the mother began to make excuses, to tell of the embarrassment it would cause the family, the phone clicked.

A few hours later the mother answered the phone again. The police sergeant at the other end said, "We have found the body of a boy with one arm, one leg, one eye, and a mangled face; he just killed himself with a shot in the head. The identification papers on the body say he is your son."

It's too bad this young man had not called Mary, a woman I know who owns a small, unattractive house on an unremarkable street in Kansas City. The front porch is a junkyard of patio furniture and chairs rusting at the joints. Inside, visitors are confronted by unpleasant smells, and stacks of books, records, and dirty dishes. Cardboard is stacked in the hole of the TV, which once held a picture tube.

Mary calls the house her "miracle house" because she believes the Lord helped her get it. But it is a miracle house in other ways as well. Since 1972 Mary has taken in over 100

troubled people—human driftwood washed up on the shores of the inner city. They have included alcoholics and the severely mentally ill, the undirected and the misdirected. Sometimes her "guests" have helped with the chores; sometimes they have pilfered her meager belongings. Some have left for a job and a family; others have gone on to prison. But whatever their problems, Mary has provided food and bed, along with a testimony to her faith in Christ. Says Mary, "I feel like I am paying rent for the space I occupy on earth." Says one of her church friends, "I have never understood how Mary could be comfortable around those people."

Mary has been blind since birth.

Yes. It's too bad the disfigured Vietnam vet did not telephone Mary.

The contrast between these two stories is stunning. How do we account for the totally different responses to "the ugly"? Which spirit do we condemn, and which one do we extol? One is easily enough honored but not so easily duplicated.

Mary's story left me, a seminary professor, wanting to ask her, "How may I too exemplify the Spirit of Christ?" She is a 20th-century embodiment of those in Matthew, to whom Jesus said, "Take your inheritance, the kingdom prepared for you" (25:34). According to the standards of beauty hawked by TV and magazine advertisements, Mary is ugly. But by the standards of the Beatitudes, she is beautiful. For she loves the unlovable, the ugly.

Can we really love the ugly? What a subject! Perhaps our first impulse is to utter a nervous, on-the-run, "Sure, that's what Christians are supposed to do," and then hope we can outrun the follow-up questions. Let's not do that. Let's deal with the questions. For some people, loving the ugly seems to come naturally. For others of us, this is definitely not the case.

Who are the ugly among us? We seem to know who they are not. Christine is unforgettable; she was pitifully cross-eyed, and yet she was heaping ridicule on a classmate, a boy with a speech handicap. Who the ugly are differs from era to era, from culture to culture, and from person to person. I remember the missionary's slide of the African woman with the elongated neck, encased in a series of rings reaching from her head to her shoulders. As a small boy I laughed at the "ugly" woman, until I was stunned to learn that in her culture the rings represented wealth and beauty.

Our society also identifies the "ugly" ones. Much of this is artificially generated by the advertisers and style setters. Some of it is innocent. But all of it is serious and can have tragic consequences for the person who feels trapped in a prison of self-contempt because he or she cannot measure up to the "Mr. or Ms. Perfect" displayed in advertisements and on television screens.

Some "Christian" television programs baptize this artificial image of beauty by parading America's "beautiful" and "successful" people as models of the essence of Christian faith and life. The practice is scandalously misleading. It is an idolatrous mimicking of the world's reduction of truth and beauty to the material and the physical.

Christians ought to be wise enough to see through the image of fake beauty generated by the ad man's need to sell hair spray, cars, girdles, and skin creams. If we can't rise above this gaudiness, if we can't see the error of reducing people to the cut of their clothes and the style of their car, then we should probably take a close look at why we even bother to call ourselves Christians.

Who Are the Ugly?

But there are other people by whom we are repelled, the reasons for which we cannot afford to ignore. There are people whose physical features are so disproportionate or misformed that they strike us as offensive, frightening, and a cause for evasion. Try as we might, we can't deny the fact. The same is often true of those who have serious mental handicaps that affect their behavior and appearance. And what about the person whose lack of basic social graces makes us extremely uncomfortable?

There is also a certain ugliness that attaches itself to the person who has "failure" written all over him, and who usually doesn't seem to know it. He has failed at selling insurance, raising earthworms, and hawking Tupperware. Not to worry; he is about to make $1 million selling snow skis at airports in Florida!

We haven't mentioned those people whose faces and personalities have through the years been deeply etched by hate, anger, pessimism, greed, or lust. While we may be inclined to smile at the "snow ski tycoon," we don't normally grant such an indulgence to these people.

And then there are the people who have made themselves ugly through the use of drugs, which have warped their bodies and twisted their personalities. We impulsively turn from them.

Our cities harbor large populations of other ugly people—the street people, often destitute beyond our comprehension. Most of us are at least tempted to ask, "What did they do to get themselves in that condition?" The list of the social outcasts could be extended, but the point is made: There are ugly people in our world, and most of us recoil at the sight of them.

Often we avoid ugly people because we don't know how to respond to them. They make us uncomfortable, and we want to avoid embarrassment and discomfort. Most often, no disrespect is intended. We just don't know what to do. Also, most of us crave "normalcy"—to be like those we know and respect—and we tend to maneuver around abnormal circumstances and people that jeopardize it. The ugly may also remind us of how tenuous is our hold on normalcy. For they can call into question our very definition of what should and should not be called "normal."

For many people, avoiding the ugly seems to be a way to

satisfy and maintain the purity of their ideals. But not for Christians, whose God has a long and remarkable history of loving the ugly. In fact, when we talk about how God loves the unlovely, we say most of what we know about Him. And when we talk about how He loves the unlovely, we have said most of what we know about ourselves.

Think of it! The God who created the heavens and the earth, who has the grandeur of Bach and the Andes to His credit, also identifies with the outcasts, those recognized by the dominant society as ugly. He regularly identified with slaves, widows, and orphans. And in the New Testament, in Christ, God embraced tax collectors, Samaritans, the demon possessed, and the crippled. Even a prostitute and an adulteress were given reason to hope, to rejoice. And "while we were yet sinners, Christ died for us" (Romans 5:8, KJV).

Why all this? Because not only was He Creator once upon a time, but also He continues to create, to give life. As the Redeemer He is the Re-creator, the God of grace and restoration. In unconditional love He acted to undo the effects of sin upon the world. With forgiveness, healing, and reconciliation He confronted the ugliness of sin, which is repulsive beyond human comprehension. And miracle of miracles, He succeeded and continues to succeed.

Christians, the apostle Paul said, should no longer evaluate people according to worldly standards, but according to the measure of God's grace (2 Corinthians 5:16). The value of a person is given by God, and not by the shifting whims of society.

Measuring people's value according to God's standards is where Christians part company with the world. It is at this point of departure that we begin loving the unlovely, the ugly. Such love becomes possible when God's love is expressed through us, not as a human love that is based simply on the appealing, pleasant, rewarding features of another. You and I can become agents of transformation when we extend to others God's valuation of them.

How Can We Love the Ugly?

This moves the discussion from *why* we ought to love the ugly to *how* we can love the ugly.

This doesn't mean that all of a sudden the unattractive becomes attractive. But rather, it means that the unattractive, though painfully real and discomforting, is transcended. We move beyond the surface images. Mother Teresa of India is a remarkable contemporary example of this. Working daily with the poor and dying of Calcutta, she sees the figure of Jesus Christ in every person who reaches out for help.

Many of us are largely insulated from the ugly people of society. As a result, they exist as a phantom, a specter to be feared and avoided. Many of us have little opportunity to see the form of Christ in those who hunger, are homeless, or are institutionalized. For some years I have taken seminary students to visit the "Lifers' Club" at the Lansing State Penitentiary in Lansing, Kans. Almost always the response is, "For the first time I recognize that prisoners are *really people,* with hopes and fears just as I have."

There are many opportunities in most areas of the country for people to do volunteer work in food pantries, prisons, homes for the aged, soup kitchens, shelters for abused children and spouses, and halfway houses. All of these present opportunities to help other people raise their own estimate of self-worth. And they also remove us from our isolation and reluctance to reach out to the unattractive.

We must look for and act upon opportunities to demonstrate God's love even to the ugly. This requires a deliberate and sometimes emotionally costly investment. But here the investment need not result in a similar response, or "return on investment," from the ugly. The investment is successful just because it is done in Jesus' name. However, it may also pay the dividend of opening "the ugly" to a measure of hope, joy, community, and personal fulfillment they have never known before.

In our world there are many people like that Vietnam vet who wanted to bring home "a friend," people who want to be accepted as creations of God who are valued by Him. "Home" for this person may be nothing more than our smile of acceptance, our words of patience, or our demonstration of respect. There are plenty of opportunities in this world for us to remind people of the value God attaches to them.

Maybe it will help motivate us to do more of this if we remind ourselves that to love the unlovely is to make the kind of investment in others that Christ made in us.

Al Truesdale is professor of Christian ethics at Nazarene Theological Seminary, Kansas City.

Chapter 13

Healed Helpers

by David A. Seamands

Background Scripture: Romans 8:18-28; 2 Corinthians 12:9-10

I ONCE VISITED A CITY where they had a great recycling plant for garbage. In this recycling plant the garbage was turned into useful fuel for energy. In a similar way God's recycling grace takes our infirmities, our damaged emotions, and the garbage of our lives and turns them from curses that cripple into means for growth and instruments to be used in His service.

There is no place in Scripture that deals with this more profoundly or beautifully than Romans 8:18-28. While this passage certainly has a wider application, I want to apply it particularly to the way God can change people who are hurting into healed helpers.

Paul began by recognizing the fact that we live in a fallen, imperfect, and suffering world. Immediately, some-one may object: "I get tired of you preachers always falling back on this. Why does there have to be so much pain and suffering in this world?"

The important words in that protest are *this world,* and they are precisely Paul's point. We suffer because it is *this world,* not some dream world that we would like to have, some utopia that we may fantasize about and wish to live in. We live in *this world*—after the Fall, this side of Eden, this paradise-lost world where sin entered by the choices of God's children. In *this world* where evil spoiled God's original perfect blueprint: marred it, scarred it, defaced and disfigured it. In *this world,* where now, instead of God's perfect and intentional will, we often—perhaps always—have to

settle for His permissive and conditional will. Paul was really saying, "Face reality! You cannot push history back before the Fall; you cannot live in a dream world."

If we were able to trace all human damages and hurts, we would find that ultimately they are the result of someone's sin, perhaps even generations back.

So often when someone in my office has been pouring out a fearful story of hurts, he will stop and say, "But one of the things that helped is that later I got to know his or her parents or grandparents, the family. I found out what happened to him and how damaged and destroyed he was. Then I began to understand and even to feel compassion." I am always glad to hear that, for I know that compassion can bring acceptance, and acceptance can give birth to love.

The One Alongside

Paul applied this profound theology to a very practical area—the place where we live with our damaged emotions and hangups. "The Holy Spirit helps us in our infirmities," in our weaknesses (see Romans 8:26, KJV). Thank God! He doesn't leave us alone; we are not abandoned to our paltry resources to somehow struggle through all this mess, to live defeated lives. No! For our Wounded Healer, our High Priest, Jesus Christ, is "touched with the feeling of our infirmities" (Hebrews 4:15, KJV). Jesus, the Son of God, identified with us humans when He became the Son of Man. He not only knows our infirmities, but also our feelings. He understands the pain of rejection, the anxiety of separation, the terror of loneliness and abandonment.

Because Christ is the Wounded Healer, because He does fully understand, when He got ready to leave this world, He promised that He would not leave His friends alone, but would come to them by sending the Comforter. "I will send you One whom you can call upon who will come alongside and *help* you with your infirmities" (see John 14:16-18).

And how does the Holy Spirit help us with these crippling infirmities? "For we do not know how to pray as we should, but the Spirit Himself intercedes for us" (Romans 8:26, NASB). Only the Holy Spirit truly knows the mind of God. And only the Holy Spirit truly understands us. Because He understands the inside of us and understands the inside of the heart of God, He knows how to get these two together. And so the Spirit himself intercedes for us with groanings too deep to be uttered. He intercedes for us in agreement with the will of God.

"He who searches the hearts knows what the mind of the Spirit is" (v. 27, NASB). If you will take the word *hearts* and roughly translate it "subconscious minds," I think you will understand what Paul was saying. In this deep inner self—this great storehouse of our memories where our hurts lie buried too deep for ordinary prayer—this is where emotional healing takes place by the work of the Holy Spirit. This is where the soothing Balm of Gilead repairs damages, and pours in the love of God to bring healing. The Comforter not only comes alongside, but He also comes inside.

Too often we quote Romans 8:28 out of context. It is the final step in this whole corrective sequence: "And we know that God causes all things to work together for good to those who love God" (NASB). The older version of this verse can be misleading: "All things work together for good . . ." (KJV). Unfortunately the *things* do not; they may even work against us. But *God* works in and through the things, causing circumstances to work out for our good. That's different, for it turns the emphasis from fate to a Father! That God causes all things to work together for good is the greatest part of the entire healing process.

Without this, the healing could not be considered total, for total healing is more than soothing painful memories, more than forgiving and being forgiven of harmful resentments, even more than the reprogramming of our minds. Healing is the miracle of God's recycling grace, where He takes it all and makes good come out of it, where He actually recycles our hangups into usefulness.

Betty

Betty and her husband came to counsel with me. I knew that they were a deeply committed Christian couple preparing for Christian service, and that they had a solid marriage. However, recently there had been some relational difficulties between them and an increasing sense of depression on Betty's part. Her tears flowed freely that first time we met together—tears which surprised her. She thought she had turned them off many years ago, but now they seemed to turn themselves on, uncontrollably and embarrassingly.

When Betty came back the next time, she began to share her story with me. Her parents had been forced to get married because her mother was pregnant with her. It was an undesired marriage and Betty had been unwanted. (May I just say parenthetically that if this is true of your life, then sometime you need to come to peaceful terms with it.)

When Betty was three and a half, her mother became pregnant again. However, her father had impregnated another woman at about the same time. This led to serious conflict and finally to divorce. Betty's memory of all this was incredibly clear. She vividly remembered that final day when her father walked out the door and left home. She remembered being in her own little crib-bed in the room when it happened; hearing the vicious quarrel and the terrifying moment when he left. It had left an aching, malignant core of pain deep within her. It was while we were in the midst of reexperiencing that incident during a time of prayer for the healing of her memories, that the Lord took us right back into that crib.

During that healing time, Betty uttered a wracking, wrenching cry of pain which had been buried for many years. I said to her, "Betty, if you could have said something to your father from your crib, at that moment—what would you have said?" And suddenly the Holy Spirit brought back up into her memory exactly what she had felt in that moment of total desolation. And she cried out, not in the voice of a young adult, but with the sobs of a three-and-a-half-year-old, "Oh Daddy, please don't leave me!" And all the terror and the pain of that moment came out "with sounds too deep to be uttered."

Later, as we prayed together, it dawned on me that if we were to translate Christ's cry of dereliction from the Cross ("My God, My God, why hast Thou forsaken Me?") into a paraphrase for a child, we couldn't improve on Betty's words: "Daddy, please don't leave me!" And suddenly, I realized that because of what Jesus experienced on that Cross, He understands the cries heard so often in our day, the cries of millions of little children, "Daddy," or "Mommy, please don't leave me!" But they *do* leave. And the Wounded Healer understands those cries and is touched with the feelings of those children.

This was the beginning of a profound healing in Betty's life. However, I wanted her to experience the ultimate wholeness promised in Romans 8:28. So we talked about trying to understand the meaning of her life. Where was God when she began life itself? Had she made peace with the circumstances of her birth through an unwanted pregnancy? She said she hadn't.

I felt led to give her a strange assignment, one I've given out only a few times in all my counseling years. I said, "Betty, I am going to give you some homework and I want you to spend time meditating and praying about it. I want you to imagine the very moment of your conception. Imagine that particular time when one cell of life from your father broke into the living cell of your mother, and *you* came into existence. That's when *you* broke into human history. As you think about that, ask yourself one question: *where was God at that moment?*"

Betty took her assignment seriously. When we met one week later, she told me what had happened: "You know, the first two or three days, I really thought this whole thing was crazy. The only thing I could think of was a verse of Scripture which kept coming to my mind, 'In sin did my mother conceive me.' But about the third day when I was reluctantly meditating on it, I began to cry. But it was a different cry than usual. A prayer was welling up from way down inside me, and I wrote it down."

She handed it to me, and with her permission I share it with you:

O God, my heart leaps with the thought that You, my loving Father, have never forsaken me. You were there when I was conceived in earthly lust. You looked upon me with a Father's love even then. You were thinking of me in my mother's womb, planning in Your divine knowledge the person I was to become, molding me in Your image.

Knowing the pain in store, You gave me a mind that would pull me above the hurt, until in Your own timing You could heal me.

You were there when my mother gave birth to me, looking on in tenderness, standing in the vacant place of my father. You were there when I cried the bitter tears of a child whose father had abandoned her. You were holding me in Your arms all the while, rocking me gently in Your soothing love.

Oh, why did I not know of Your presence? Even as a child I was blind to Your love, unable to know it in its depth and breadth.

God, my dear, dear Father, my heart had turned to frost, but the light of Your love is beginning to warm it. I can feel again. You have begun to work in me a healing miracle. I trust You and I praise You. Your goodness and mercy have been with me always. Your love has never left me. And now the eyes of my soul have been opened. I see You for who You really are, my true Father. I know Your love and now I am ready to forgive. Please make the healing complete.

Betty had found the final stage of healing, when God took all the hurts she gave Him and healed them by His recycling and healing love. But then God put the frosting on the cake—He used Betty as a healed helper.

One Sunday morning I did something in my sermon that I rarely do. With Betty's express permission I used the above story. I disguised details that would identify her, since I knew she would be in the congregation. At the end of the service I invited people to come forward to the front altar if they desired prayer for emotional healing. A large number responded. Betty was seated next to a friend who began to weep profusely during the time of invitation, but who did not go forward. Betty moved closer, and putting her arm around her friend, asked if she would like her to go with her and pray for her. The lady was very hesitant, and protested that her problems were too deep and that Betty wouldn't really understand.

Now there took place within Betty a real struggle: she knew what she *thought* God was asking her to do, and she thought He was asking a little too much! But within minutes she knew what she had to do. So she leaned over and whispered in her friend's ear, "Don't be shocked: I gave Dr. Seamands permission to tell that story this morning: you see, *I'm Betty!*" Her friend looked at her incredulously.

"Yes," she said again, "I'm Betty, and I think I can understand and maybe help." They came forward together and spent a long time talking and praying. This was the beginning of a healing in the life of Betty's friend. When Betty related it to me, she had the glow of a healed helper. God had truly recycled her hurts into healing and helpfulness!

The Other Alongside

Too many of us think that we can only minister out of strength—that only when we are victorious and can impress people with our strong points will we bring God the most glory. But Paul claimed that there are only two things we can glory in. The first is the cross of Christ (Galatians 6:14), perhaps the ultimate place of weakness in all human history, the last word in injustice, which God turned into the salvation of the whole world. The other thing in which we can glory is our infirmities, or weaknesses (2 Corinthians 12:9-10). Why? Because God's strength is made perfect in our weakness. As Christians we are called to be healed helpers, moving not out of strength, but out of weakness.

Often in the counseling room someone will share very deep problems or perplexities. There is always the temptation to impress him, to be the wise counselor, to move from strength and give good advice.

But then the Holy Spirit whispers, "David, share yourself with this person. This is not a 'client,' not a 'case' (I hate that term!); this is a hurting human being. Let him in on your infirmities, your damaged emotions, and your struggles. Share with him how the Spirit has helped you in your weaknesses."

Often I inwardly resist and argue with the Spirit: "But Lord, I can't do that, because he has come to me as the pastor. He respects me; he sees me as strong and wise and having all the answers."

In time, I usually yield to His gentle pressure and follow His instructions. And every time I do, this promise of 2 Corinthians 12:9-10 comes alive, as God has a chance to exercise His power, and as His strength is made perfect in and through my weakness.

Again and again I have been a part of this deep healing as God recycles the damages, the pains, and the infirmities and then uses them for someone's good and His glory.

What I have experienced in my own life, I have seen take place in the lives of many others. I dare to believe it can also happen in your life!

Condensed by permission from *Healing for Damaged Emotions,* by David A. Seamands. Published by Victor Books and © 1981 by SP Publications, Wheaton, Ill.